John von Neumann

The Forgotten Tech Genius – Unauthorized

Aldo Omar

ISBN: 9781779699824
Imprint: Telephasic Workshop
Copyright © 2024 Aldo Omar.
All Rights Reserved.

Contents

Introduction   1
The Birth of a Genius   1

The Pioneer of Computer Science   15
The Princeton Years   15

The Father of Artificial Intelligence   27
Early Experiments in AI   27

Beyond Computer Science: Interdisciplinary Innovations   39
Contributions to Physics   39

The Unconventional Mind   53
Personal Life: Eccentricities and Relationships   53

Controversies and Forgotten Legacy   65
Neumann's Political Activism   65

Remembering the Forgotten Genius   79
Academic Institutions and Honors   79

Index   91

Introduction

The Birth of a Genius

Early Life and Education

John von Neumann was born on December 28, 1903, in Budapest, Hungary, into a well-to-do Jewish family. His father, Miklós Neumann, was a banker, while his mother, Margit Weiss, was a talented pianist. From a young age, John exhibited extraordinary intellectual abilities. By the age of six, he was already fluent in both Hungarian and German, and his prodigious talent for mathematics was evident early on.

Childhood Prodigy

Von Neumann's childhood was marked by a voracious curiosity and a remarkable aptitude for numbers. Family anecdotes describe how he could perform complex calculations in his head, astonishing adults with his speed and accuracy. For instance, when asked to multiply two large numbers, he would often provide the answer before the question was fully articulated. This early demonstration of mathematical prowess laid the groundwork for his future achievements.

Formal Education

In 1911, von Neumann began attending the *Piaristán* school, where he excelled in mathematics and science. His teachers quickly recognized his exceptional capabilities and nurtured his talents. At the age of 14, he enrolled at the *Budapest University of Technology and Economics*, where he was exposed to higher mathematics and the burgeoning field of theoretical physics.

The environment of intellectual rigor at the university played a significant role in shaping his analytical thinking. It was during this time that von Neumann encountered the works of prominent mathematicians such as David Hilbert and Henri Poincaré. The influence of these figures would resonate throughout his career.

Higher Education

In 1921, von Neumann was admitted to the *University of Budapest*, where he pursued a degree in mathematics. He completed his doctorate in 1926 at the age of 23, presenting a dissertation on *set theory* that would later contribute to the foundation of modern mathematical logic. His thesis was supervised by the renowned mathematician László Rátz, who recognized von Neumann's potential and encouraged him to explore various mathematical fields.

During his time at the university, von Neumann also studied chemistry and physics, broadening his understanding of the scientific principles that would later inform his work in computer science and artificial intelligence. His interdisciplinary approach was a hallmark of his intellectual development, allowing him to draw connections between disparate fields.

Influential Mentors

Von Neumann's education was further enriched by his interactions with notable mathematicians and physicists of the time. He spent time at the *University of Göttingen*, where he encountered the likes of Carl Friedrich Gauss and David Hilbert. These encounters not only deepened his mathematical knowledge but also instilled in him a sense of ambition and intellectual rigor.

In particular, his relationship with Hilbert was pivotal. Hilbert's formalism and emphasis on axiomatic systems influenced von Neumann's own approach to mathematics. The concept of *Hilbert space*, which became fundamental in quantum mechanics, would later be integral to von Neumann's work in physics and computer science.

Early Interests in Computing

While pursuing his studies, von Neumann developed an interest in the emerging field of computing. In the 1930s, he began to explore the potential of machines to perform calculations more efficiently than humans. His fascination with the idea of automating mathematical processes was a precursor to his later contributions to computer science.

During this period, he also engaged with the early concepts of algorithms and computation. He studied the work of Alan Turing and others who were laying the groundwork for what would become modern computer science. This early exposure to computational theory would prove crucial as he later developed the von Neumann architecture, a foundational model for computer design.

Conclusion

John von Neumann's early life and education were characterized by an extraordinary blend of talent, ambition, and intellectual curiosity. His formative years in Budapest, combined with rigorous academic training and influential mentorship, set the stage for his future as a pioneering figure in mathematics, physics, and computer science. The foundations he laid during this period would not only shape his career but also leave an indelible mark on the technological landscape of the 20th century and beyond.

Mathematical Genius Emerges

John von Neumann's journey into the realm of mathematics began at an early age, marked by an insatiable curiosity and an extraordinary aptitude for numerical reasoning. His childhood was filled with instances that hinted at his prodigious talent, as he effortlessly grasped complex concepts that would baffle many adults. This section explores the pivotal moments in von Neumann's early mathematical development, the theories that shaped his thinking, and the problems he tackled that foreshadowed his future contributions to the field.

Early Mathematical Encounters

At the tender age of six, von Neumann demonstrated an uncanny ability to perform complex calculations in his head. His mother, recognizing his exceptional talent, nurtured his mathematical inclinations by providing him with books and engaging him in discussions about numbers and logic. One of his earliest encounters with mathematics involved the concept of *combinatorics*, which deals with counting, arrangement, and combination of objects.

For instance, consider the problem of arranging three distinct objects, say A, B, and C. The total number of arrangements (permutations) can be calculated using the factorial function:

$$P(n) = n! = n \times (n-1) \times (n-2) \times \ldots \times 1$$

For $n = 3$:

$$P(3) = 3! = 3 \times 2 \times 1 = 6$$

The six arrangements of the objects A, B, and C are: ABC, ACB, BAC, BCA, CAB, and CBA. This early fascination with counting and arrangements laid the groundwork for von Neumann's later work in game theory and probability.

Influence of Mentors

Von Neumann's formal education at the Budapest University of Technology and Economics introduced him to influential mathematicians such as *László Kalmár* and *János Bolyai*. Kalmár's teachings on set theory and mathematical logic inspired von Neumann to explore the foundations of mathematics. He quickly became adept at formal proofs, a skill that would serve him well throughout his career.

A notable example of his early work in logic is the *Principle of Mathematical Induction*, a fundamental proof technique used to establish the truth of an infinite number of cases. This principle can be summarized as follows:

1. Prove that the statement is true for the base case (usually $n = 1$). 2. Assume the statement is true for $n = k$. 3. Prove that the statement is true for $n = k + 1$.

If both steps are satisfied, the statement is true for all natural numbers n.

The Birth of Abstract Thinking

As von Neumann progressed in his studies, he began to develop an interest in *abstract algebra* and the structures that govern mathematical systems. He was particularly fascinated by the concept of *groups*, which are sets equipped with an operation that satisfies certain axioms. The group theory, which later became a cornerstone of modern mathematics, allows for the study of symmetrical structures and has applications in various fields, including physics and chemistry.

An example of a simple group is the set of integers under addition. The group $(\mathbb{Z}, +)$ satisfies the following properties:

1. **Closure:** For any $a, b \in \mathbb{Z}$, $a + b \in \mathbb{Z}$. 2. **Associativity:** For any $a, b, c \in \mathbb{Z}$, $(a + b) + c = a + (b + c)$. 3. **Identity Element:** There exists an element $0 \in \mathbb{Z}$ such that $a + 0 = a$ for all $a \in \mathbb{Z}$. 4. **Inverse Element:** For each $a \in \mathbb{Z}$, there exists an element $-a \in \mathbb{Z}$ such that $a + (-a) = 0$.

This early exposure to abstract concepts would later enable von Neumann to tackle complex problems in various mathematical domains.

The Impact of Competition

Von Neumann's competitive spirit was evident during his time at the university. He thrived in an environment where intellectual prowess was highly valued, often engaging in mathematical challenges with his peers. One such challenge involved solving *differential equations*, which are equations that relate a function to its derivatives.

For example, consider the simple first-order differential equation:

$$\frac{dy}{dx} = ky$$

where k is a constant. The solution to this equation can be found using the method of separation of variables:

$$\frac{dy}{y} = k\,dx$$

Integrating both sides yields:

$$\ln|y| = kx + C \quad \Rightarrow \quad y = Ce^{kx}$$

This equation models exponential growth or decay, a concept that von Neumann would later apply in various scientific fields, including economics and population dynamics.

Conclusion

By the time von Neumann completed his education, he had not only mastered the fundamentals of mathematics but had also laid the foundation for his future innovations. His early experiences with combinatorics, logic, group theory, and differential equations shaped his approach to problem-solving and provided him with the tools necessary to become one of the most influential mathematicians of the 20th century.

As we delve deeper into von Neumann's life, it becomes clear that his mathematical genius was not merely a product of innate talent but also a result of the rich tapestry of experiences, mentors, and challenges that defined his formative years.

Influential Mentors and Teachers

John von Neumann's journey from a prodigious child to a leading figure in mathematics and computer science was significantly shaped by the influential mentors and teachers he encountered throughout his early life and education. These figures not only recognized his extraordinary talent but also nurtured his intellectual curiosity, leading him to explore various fields that would later define his groundbreaking contributions.

The Early Influences

Von Neumann was born in Budapest in 1903, a city that was a hub of intellectual activity. His early education took place at the Lutheran Secondary School, where he was introduced to a variety of subjects, including mathematics, languages, and the sciences. Here, he was first inspired by his mathematics teacher, **László Rátz**, who recognized von Neumann's exceptional abilities. Rátz encouraged him to explore advanced mathematical concepts, fostering a love for the subject that would last a lifetime.

$$\text{Mathematical Curiosity} = f(\text{Encouragement from Rátz}) + g(\text{Exposure to Advanced Concepts}) \tag{1}$$

Rátz's influence was pivotal, but it was von Neumann's later studies at the **University of Budapest** that truly expanded his horizons. Here, he was exposed to a broader array of mathematical disciplines and ideas, particularly through the teachings of **Gyula Kőnig**, who was instrumental in introducing von Neumann to set theory and logic.

A Formative Experience in Berlin

In 1921, von Neumann moved to Berlin to continue his studies at the **University of Berlin**. This transition marked a significant turning point in his intellectual development. He had the opportunity to attend lectures by some of the most prominent mathematicians of the time, including **David Hilbert** and **Hermann Weyl**. Hilbert's work on mathematical foundations and formalism left a profound impact on von Neumann, particularly his famous *Hilbert's Problems*, which sought to address the unsolved questions in mathematics.

$$\text{Hilbert's Problems} \implies \text{Inspiration for Future Research} \tag{2}$$

Hilbert's emphasis on rigorous proofs and the formalization of mathematics resonated with von Neumann, shaping his approach to mathematical logic and set theory. He later contributed to these fields, notably through his work on the **Hilbert space** concept, which became foundational in quantum mechanics.

THE BIRTH OF A GENIUS

The Influence of American Academia

In 1926, von Neumann moved to the United States, where he began teaching at **Princeton University**. His arrival coincided with a period of rapid development in mathematical sciences, and he quickly became a central figure in the academic community. At Princeton, he encountered influential figures such as **Oswald Veblen** and **John Tukey**, who played crucial roles in shaping his ideas and research.

$$\text{Collaboration} = \text{Veblen} + \text{Tukey} + \text{von Neumann} \qquad (3)$$

Veblen's work in topology and geometry provided von Neumann with new perspectives on mathematical structures, while Tukey's contributions to statistics and data analysis influenced von Neumann's later work in game theory and computer science.

Game Theory and Strategic Thinking

One of the most significant relationships von Neumann developed during this period was with **John Nash**. Although Nash was a student rather than a mentor, their interactions were mutually beneficial. Nash's groundbreaking work in game theory, which von Neumann had laid the groundwork for, led to a deeper exploration of strategic decision-making and mathematical modeling.

$$\text{Nash Equilibrium} = \text{Optimal Strategy for Players} \qquad (4)$$

Von Neumann's collaboration with Nash culminated in the publication of *Theory of Games and Economic Behavior*, a foundational text that established game theory as a vital area of study in both mathematics and economics.

Conclusion

In summary, John von Neumann's intellectual development was profoundly influenced by a series of mentors and teachers who recognized and nurtured his extraordinary talents. From Rátz's early encouragement in Budapest to the profound impact of Hilbert and his peers in Berlin and Princeton, these figures shaped von Neumann's approach to mathematics, logic, and computer science. Their guidance not only helped him navigate the complexities of these fields but also inspired him to push the boundaries of knowledge, ultimately leading to his status as one of the most significant figures in the history of technology and science.

The legacy of these mentors can be seen in von Neumann's contributions to various disciplines, as he synthesized their teachings into a unique and innovative perspective that would pave the way for future generations of thinkers and innovators.

$$\text{Legacy of Mentorship} = \sum_{i=1}^{n} \text{Influence}_i \qquad (5)$$

Developing an Interest in Computers

John von Neumann's fascination with computers can be traced back to the early 1940s, a time when the world was on the brink of technological revolution. As the Second World War raged on, the need for advanced computational tools became increasingly apparent. The war effort demanded rapid calculations, complex simulations, and the processing of vast amounts of data, which traditional methods could not efficiently handle. It was during this period that von Neumann's interest in machines capable of performing these tasks began to blossom.

The Concept of a Stored-Program Computer

One of the pivotal moments in von Neumann's journey into the realm of computing was his development of the concept of a stored-program computer. Prior to this innovation, computers were primarily designed to execute a single task, with programs hardwired into the machinery. Von Neumann proposed a revolutionary idea: a computer could store both data and instructions in its memory, allowing it to perform a variety of tasks without the need for physical reconfiguration.

The architecture that emerged from this concept is now known as the **von Neumann architecture**. This model consists of five primary components:

- **Memory:** Stores data and instructions.

- **Control Unit:** Directs the operation of the processor and its interaction with memory.

- **Arithmetic Logic Unit (ALU):** Performs mathematical calculations and logical operations.

- **Input/Output (I/O) Devices:** Facilitate communication between the computer and the outside world.

- **Bus System:** Transfers data between the components.

The significance of this architecture cannot be overstated. It laid the foundation for virtually all modern computers, enabling them to execute complex programs with remarkable efficiency.

The ENIAC and the Influence of the Manhattan Project

As von Neumann's interest in computing deepened, he became involved in the development of the **Electronic Numerical Integrator and Computer (ENIAC)**, one of the first general-purpose electronic computers. ENIAC was designed to calculate artillery firing tables for the United States Army during World War II. Its construction was a monumental task, requiring the collaboration of several brilliant minds, including John Mauchly and J. Presper Eckert.

Von Neumann's role in the project was crucial. He recognized that the ENIAC's potential extended far beyond military applications. His insights into the need for programmability and flexibility in computing systems were instrumental in shaping the machine's design. In 1945, he authored the *First Draft of a Report on the EDVAC*, which outlined the principles of the stored-program architecture, solidifying his position as a pioneer in computer science.

The impact of the Manhattan Project also played a significant role in von Neumann's fascination with computing. The project's demands for rapid calculations in nuclear physics and engineering further fueled his interest. The collaboration with physicists and engineers exposed him to the practical applications of computing in solving complex problems, reinforcing the idea that machines could enhance human capabilities.

Theoretical Foundations and Early Algorithms

Von Neumann's interest in computers was not solely driven by practical applications; it was also rooted in his deep understanding of mathematical theories. He began to explore the theoretical foundations of computing, delving into algorithms and their efficiency. One of his notable contributions was the development of the **minimax theorem**, a fundamental concept in game theory that has implications in computer science, particularly in artificial intelligence.

The minimax theorem states that in a two-player, zero-sum game, there exists a strategy that minimizes the possible loss for a worst-case scenario. This concept laid the groundwork for algorithmic decision-making in computing, influencing the design of algorithms used in various applications, including artificial intelligence and optimization problems.

The Birth of Game Theory and Its Connection to Computers

Von Neumann's exploration of game theory was closely intertwined with his burgeoning interest in computers. His collaboration with Oskar Morgenstern led to the publication of *Theory of Games and Economic Behavior* in 1944, a seminal work that introduced the mathematical framework for analyzing strategic interactions among rational decision-makers.

The principles of game theory have far-reaching implications in computer science, particularly in the development of algorithms for competitive environments. Von Neumann's insights into strategic decision-making informed the design of algorithms that simulate competitive scenarios, laying the groundwork for advancements in fields such as artificial intelligence, economics, and operations research.

The Legacy of von Neumann's Early Work in Computing

The culmination of von Neumann's early work in computing set the stage for the rapid advancements that would follow. His contributions to the field were not limited to theoretical frameworks; they also encompassed practical implementations that shaped the trajectory of computer science.

The establishment of the **Institute for Advanced Study** in Princeton provided von Neumann with a platform to further explore his interests in computing. His collaborations with other brilliant minds, including Alan Turing, fostered an environment of innovation that propelled the field forward. Von Neumann's vision of a world where machines could augment human intelligence became a driving force behind the development of early computers and laid the foundation for the future of artificial intelligence.

In conclusion, von Neumann's early interest in computers was a confluence of practical necessity, theoretical exploration, and collaborative innovation. His pioneering contributions to the concept of stored-program computers, game theory, and algorithm design not only advanced the field of computer science but also left an indelible mark on the technological landscape of the 20th century. As we reflect on his legacy, it is clear that John von Neumann was not just a mathematician or a physicist; he was a visionary who recognized the transformative power of machines and their potential to reshape the world.

World War II and the Manhattan Project

The Second World War was not merely a backdrop for John von Neumann's life; it was a crucible that tested his intellect and shaped his legacy. As the specter of

THE BIRTH OF A GENIUS

global conflict loomed, von Neumann's mathematical prowess and innovative thinking became invaluable assets to the United States. His work during this tumultuous period would not only impact the war effort but also lay the groundwork for future scientific endeavors.

The Call to Arms

In the early 1940s, as the United States entered World War II, the urgency for scientific advancements became palpable. Von Neumann, already a prominent mathematician, was drawn into the war effort through his connections with the Manhattan Project. This top-secret initiative aimed to develop the first atomic bomb, a project that would require the collaboration of the brightest minds in physics, mathematics, and engineering.

Mathematical Contributions

Von Neumann's contributions to the Manhattan Project were multifaceted. He applied his expertise in various mathematical fields, particularly in hydrodynamics and shock wave theory, to address the complex problems associated with nuclear explosions. One of the critical challenges was understanding the behavior of explosive materials under extreme conditions.

The mathematical model he developed for the detonation of nuclear materials can be described by the following equation, which relates pressure, density, and the speed of sound in the explosive medium:

$$P = \rho c^2 \tag{6}$$

Where:

- P is the pressure,

- ρ is the density, and

- c is the speed of sound in the medium.

This equation illustrates how von Neumann's work bridged theoretical mathematics and practical applications in explosive dynamics, allowing scientists to predict the behavior of nuclear reactions with unprecedented accuracy.

Collaboration with Oppenheimer and Feynman

At Los Alamos, von Neumann collaborated closely with other key figures, including J. Robert Oppenheimer, the project's scientific director, and Richard Feynman, a fellow physicist known for his work in quantum mechanics. Their discussions often revolved around the implications of their discoveries, not just for the war, but for humanity at large.

Von Neumann's ability to communicate complex mathematical ideas to a diverse group of scientists was instrumental in fostering a collaborative environment. His lectures often included practical demonstrations of theoretical concepts, making them accessible to those without a strong mathematical background.

Theoretical Physics Meets Practical Application

One of von Neumann's significant contributions was in the area of computational methods. He helped develop numerical techniques that would later be essential for simulating nuclear explosions. The use of early computers, such as the ENIAC, was crucial for performing complex calculations that could not be solved analytically.

The mathematical framework for these simulations often involved solving partial differential equations (PDEs) that describe the behavior of shock waves. For example, the equations governing the propagation of shock waves can be expressed as:

$$\frac{\partial \rho}{\partial t} + \nabla \cdot (\rho \mathbf{u}) = 0 \qquad (7)$$

Where:

- ρ is the density,
- $\mathbf{u}$ is the velocity vector, and
- t is time.

These equations were pivotal in understanding how shock waves interacted with different materials, which was critical for designing the bomb's casing and ensuring its effectiveness.

Ethical Considerations and Reflections

As the project progressed, von Neumann, like many of his colleagues, grappled with the ethical implications of their work. The realization that their scientific endeavors could lead to mass destruction weighed heavily on their consciences. Von Neumann famously remarked, "In some sort of crude sense which no vulgarity, no humor, no overstatement can quite extinguish, the physicists have known sin; and this is a knowledge which they cannot lose."

This introspection highlights the duality of scientific progress: the potential for both advancement and devastation. Von Neumann's reflections on his role in the Manhattan Project would echo throughout his later work in computer science and artificial intelligence, where he often emphasized the importance of ethical considerations in technological development.

Legacy of the Manhattan Project

The culmination of the Manhattan Project was the successful detonation of the first atomic bomb in July 1945, an event that changed the course of history. Von Neumann's contributions to the project, particularly in the realms of mathematics and computation, were crucial in this monumental achievement.

The technological advancements made during this time laid the foundation for modern computing and artificial intelligence. Von Neumann's work on the architecture of electronic computers, which would later bear his name, was influenced by his experiences during the war.

In conclusion, John von Neumann's involvement in World War II and the Manhattan Project was not merely a chapter in his biography; it was a defining moment that shaped his legacy. His ability to apply mathematical concepts to real-world problems, coupled with his ethical reflections, established him as a pivotal figure in the evolution of science and technology. As we remember von Neumann, we must also consider the lessons learned from this period, as they continue to resonate in today's discussions on technology and morality.

The Pioneer of Computer Science

The Princeton Years

Joining the Institute for Advanced Study

In 1933, John von Neumann made a pivotal decision that would shape the course of his career and the future of mathematics and computer science. He accepted a position at the Institute for Advanced Study (IAS) in Princeton, New Jersey, a haven for intellectuals and a sanctuary for groundbreaking research. The IAS was founded in 1930 by philanthropist Abraham Flexner and was designed to foster an environment where scholars could pursue their work free from the pressures of teaching and administrative duties. This unique setting provided von Neumann with the perfect backdrop to explore his myriad interests in mathematics, physics, and eventually, computer science.

The Atmosphere of Innovation

At the IAS, von Neumann was surrounded by some of the greatest minds of the 20th century, including mathematicians like Kurt Gödel and physicists such as Albert Einstein. This stimulating environment ignited von Neumann's creativity and encouraged interdisciplinary collaboration. His work began to flourish, as he engaged in discussions that transcended traditional boundaries. One of his notable contributions during this period was in the field of game theory, which would later gain prominence in economics and social sciences.

Game Theory: A New Frontier

Von Neumann's interest in game theory was not merely an academic pursuit; it was a reflection of his profound understanding of strategy and decision-making. In 1944, he co-authored the seminal book *Theory of Games and Economic Behavior* with Oskar Morgenstern, which laid the groundwork for modern game theory. The book introduced the concept of the **minimax theorem**, which states that in a zero-sum game, the optimal strategy minimizes the possible loss for a worst-case scenario. Mathematically, this can be expressed as:

$$\min_{x \in X} \max_{y \in Y} f(x, y) \tag{8}$$

where $f(x, y)$ represents the payoff function, X is the set of strategies for player one, and Y is the set of strategies for player two. The implications of this theorem extended far beyond games, influencing economics, political science, and evolutionary biology.

The von Neumann Architecture

While at the IAS, von Neumann's visionary thinking led him to conceptualize what would later be known as the **von Neumann architecture**, a foundational model for computer design. This architecture proposed a system where a single memory space would store both data and instructions, allowing for more efficient processing. The architecture can be summarized by the following components:

- **Central Processing Unit (CPU):** The brain of the computer, responsible for executing instructions.

- **Memory:** A storage area for both data and instructions.

- **Input/Output (I/O) Devices:** Interfaces for user interaction and data exchange.

The von Neumann architecture can be represented by the following block diagram:
This model became the blueprint for most modern computers, revolutionizing the field and enabling the development of programming languages and software applications.

Collaboration with Alan Turing

During his tenure at the IAS, von Neumann also established a collaborative relationship with Alan Turing, another towering figure in the development of computer science. Turing's work on the concept of a universal machine, which could simulate any algorithm, paralleled von Neumann's ideas about computation. The two exchanged ideas that would later influence the design of early computers and the theoretical foundations of computer science.

One of their key discussions revolved around the **Church-Turing thesis**, which posits that any function that can be computed algorithmically can be computed by a Turing machine. This concept not only solidified the theoretical underpinnings of computer science but also prompted von Neumann to consider the implications of machines that could "think" and solve problems autonomously.

Impact on Future Research

The time von Neumann spent at the Institute for Advanced Study was transformative, both for him and for the fields of mathematics and computer science. His contributions during this period laid the groundwork for future innovations, including advancements in artificial intelligence and quantum computing. The IAS not only provided von Neumann with the intellectual freedom to pursue his interests but also positioned him at the forefront of a new era in scientific research.

In summary, joining the Institute for Advanced Study marked a significant turning point in von Neumann's career. The collaborative atmosphere, coupled with his groundbreaking work in game theory and computer architecture, positioned him as a leading figure in the development of modern science and technology. His legacy continues to influence generations of researchers and innovators, reminding us of the profound impact that a single mind can have on the world.

Contribution to Game Theory

Game Theory, a mathematical framework for analyzing competitive situations where the outcomes depend on the actions of multiple agents, owes much of its foundational development to John von Neumann. His pioneering work laid the groundwork for what would become a crucial area of study in economics, political science, and biology.

The Minimax Theorem

One of von Neumann's most significant contributions to Game Theory is the Minimax Theorem, which he published in 1928. The theorem provides a strategy for two-player zero-sum games, where one player's gain is equivalent to the other's loss. The formal statement of the theorem can be expressed as follows:

$$V = \max_{s \in S} \min_{t \in T} u(s,t) \tag{9}$$

Here, V represents the value of the game, S is the set of strategies available to player 1, T is the set of strategies available to player 2, and $u(s,t)$ is the utility function that denotes the outcome based on the chosen strategies of both players.

This theorem implies that in a zero-sum game, there exists a strategy for each player that can guarantee them a minimum payoff, regardless of the opponent's actions. The concept of mixed strategies, where players randomize over their available strategies, is a direct result of the Minimax Theorem.

Applications of the Minimax Theorem

The Minimax Theorem has far-reaching implications across various fields. In economics, it helps analyze competitive market situations where firms must anticipate their rivals' actions. For example, consider two companies, A and B, competing in a market. Each company can either choose to set a high price or a low price for their product. The payoff matrix might look like this:

& B: High Price & B: Low Price
A: High Price & (2, 2) & (0, 3)
A: Low Price & (3, 0) & (1, 1)

In this matrix, the first number in each pair represents the payoff for company A, while the second number represents the payoff for company B. By applying the Minimax Theorem, each firm can determine its optimal pricing strategy, considering the potential responses from its competitor.

Nash Equilibrium and Beyond

While von Neumann's work set the stage for Game Theory, it was John Nash who expanded upon these ideas in the 1950s, introducing the concept of Nash Equilibrium. A Nash Equilibrium occurs when each player's strategy is optimal, given the strategies of all other players. In a Nash Equilibrium, no player has anything to gain by changing only their own strategy.

Von Neumann's contributions provided the mathematical rigor necessary for Nash's later developments. The interplay between these two theorists highlights the evolution of Game Theory from von Neumann's foundational principles to the broader applications explored by Nash and others.

The Theory of Cooperative Games

In addition to his work on non-cooperative games, von Neumann also contributed to the theory of cooperative games, where players can form coalitions and negotiate shared payoffs. This aspect of Game Theory is crucial in understanding how groups can work together to achieve better outcomes than they would individually.

The core of cooperative game theory involves the concept of the *Shapley value*, which quantifies how to fairly distribute the total gains among players based on their contributions to the coalition. Although the Shapley value was formally introduced by Lloyd Shapley in 1953, von Neumann's early work on cooperative strategies laid the groundwork for this and similar concepts.

Conclusion

John von Neumann's contributions to Game Theory are not merely historical footnotes; they are foundational elements that continue to influence modern economics, political science, and beyond. His Minimax Theorem remains a critical tool in strategic decision-making, while his insights into cooperative strategies have paved the way for collaborative approaches in various fields. As we delve deeper into the complexities of Game Theory, it is essential to recognize von Neumann not just as a mathematician, but as a visionary who foresaw the implications of strategic interactions long before they became integral to our understanding of human behavior.

The Development of von Neumann Architecture

The von Neumann architecture, proposed by John von Neumann in the mid-20th century, is a foundational model for designing computer systems. It describes a design architecture for an electronic computer with a stored-program concept, which allows both data and program instructions to be stored in the same memory space. This section will delve into the theoretical underpinnings, the key components of the architecture, and its profound impact on the evolution of computer science.

Key Components of von Neumann Architecture

The von Neumann architecture is characterized by five main components:

- **Memory:** This is where both data and instructions are stored. It is organized in a linear fashion, allowing for random access. Each memory location is identified by a unique address.

- **Arithmetic Logic Unit (ALU):** The ALU performs all arithmetic and logical operations. It processes the data retrieved from memory and executes the instructions.

- **Control Unit (CU):** The control unit orchestrates the operations of the computer. It fetches instructions from memory, decodes them, and directs the ALU to execute them.

- **Input/Output (I/O) Devices:** These devices facilitate communication between the computer and the outside world. They allow data to be input into the system and output from it.

- **Bus System:** The bus system is a communication pathway that connects the various components of the architecture, enabling data transfer between memory, the ALU, and I/O devices.

Stored-Program Concept

The most revolutionary aspect of the von Neumann architecture is the stored-program concept. This innovation allows a computer to store a sequence of instructions in memory, enabling it to perform complex calculations and tasks without human intervention. The significance of this concept can be illustrated through the following equation representing the execution cycle:

$$\text{Execution Cycle} = \text{Fetch} + \text{Decode} + \text{Execute} + \text{Store} \qquad (10)$$

Where:

- **Fetch:** The control unit retrieves an instruction from memory.

- **Decode:** The instruction is interpreted to determine the required operation.

- **Execute:** The ALU performs the specified operation using the data.

- **Store:** The result is written back to memory or sent to an output device.

Theoretical Foundations and Implications

The theoretical underpinnings of the von Neumann architecture are rooted in mathematical logic and set theory. The architecture's ability to manipulate symbols and perform logical operations laid the groundwork for the development of programming languages and compilers, which translate human-readable code into machine code.

One of the critical issues that arose from the von Neumann architecture is the so-called "von Neumann bottleneck," which refers to the limitation in throughput between the CPU and memory. This bottleneck occurs because both instructions and data must travel through the same bus system, leading to potential delays in processing speed. The bottleneck can be mathematically represented as:

$$\text{Throughput} = \frac{\text{Data Size}}{\text{Time Taken}} \qquad (11)$$

Where a higher data size and time taken results in reduced throughput, emphasizing the need for improved memory and processing designs.

Examples of von Neumann Architecture in Practice

The first electronic computer based on the von Neumann architecture was the Electronic Numerical Integrator and Computer (ENIAC), developed in the 1940s. Although initially designed without the stored-program concept, subsequent iterations incorporated von Neumann's principles, demonstrating the versatility and effectiveness of this architecture.

Modern computers continue to utilize the von Neumann model, albeit with enhancements and optimizations. For instance, contemporary systems implement cache memory to alleviate the von Neumann bottleneck by storing frequently accessed data closer to the CPU, thereby speeding up processing times.

Conclusion

In summary, the development of the von Neumann architecture marks a pivotal moment in the history of computing. Its introduction of the stored-program concept revolutionized how computers are designed and operated, allowing for increased complexity and versatility in computational tasks. Despite challenges such as the von Neumann bottleneck, the architecture remains a fundamental framework in computer science, influencing everything from hardware design to programming paradigms. As we continue to innovate and evolve in the field of computing, the legacy of John von Neumann's architectural design endures, inspiring future generations of technologists and computer scientists.

Collaboration with Alan Turing

The collaboration between John von Neumann and Alan Turing represents a pivotal moment in the history of computer science, as both men were at the forefront of theoretical developments that would shape the future of computing. Their interactions, though not extensively documented, were characterized by a mutual respect for each other's groundbreaking work in mathematics and computation.

Foundations of Computation

Alan Turing, often hailed as the father of computer science, introduced the concept of the *Turing Machine*, a theoretical construct that formalizes the notion of computation. The Turing Machine is defined by a set of states, a tape that serves as both input and output, and a head that reads and writes symbols on the tape according to a set of rules. Formally, a Turing Machine can be described as follows:

$$\text{TM} = (Q, \Sigma, \Gamma, \delta, q_0, q_{accept}, q_{reject}) \qquad (12)$$

where:

- Q is a finite set of states,
- Σ is the input alphabet,
- Γ is the tape alphabet (which includes Σ and a blank symbol),
- δ is the transition function,
- q_0 is the initial state,
- q_{accept} and q_{reject} are the accepting and rejecting states, respectively.

Von Neumann recognized the significance of Turing's work and sought to build on it, particularly in the context of developing a practical computing machine. He proposed the *von Neumann architecture*, which laid the groundwork for modern computer design. This architecture included the concept of stored-program computers, where both data and instructions are stored in the same memory space, a revolutionary idea at the time.

Game Theory and Decision Making

In addition to their work on computation, von Neumann and Turing also intersected in the realm of game theory. Von Neumann's contributions to game theory, particularly his formulation of the *minimax theorem*, provided a mathematical framework for decision-making in competitive situations. The minimax theorem states that in zero-sum games, there exists a strategy that minimizes the maximum possible loss. Formally, if two players are involved, the strategy can be expressed as:

$$v = \max_{p \in P} \min_{q \in Q} \sum_{i,j} a_{ij} p_i q_j \tag{13}$$

where:

- v is the value of the game,
- P and Q are the strategy sets for the players,
- a_{ij} is the payoff matrix.

Turing's work in cryptanalysis during World War II, particularly his development of the Bombe machine to break the Enigma code, showcased the practical application of game theory in strategic decision-making under uncertainty. While von Neumann focused on the mathematical formulation, Turing's application of these principles in real-world scenarios illustrated their profound implications.

Theoretical Implications and Legacy

The collaboration between von Neumann and Turing was not merely about direct exchanges of ideas; it represented a confluence of their respective theories that would influence the trajectory of computer science. The intersection of their work laid the foundation for key concepts such as algorithmic complexity, computability, and artificial intelligence.

For instance, von Neumann's architecture directly influenced the design of Turing-complete programming languages, which are capable of performing any computation that a Turing Machine can. This relationship is encapsulated in the Church-Turing thesis, which posits that any computation that can be performed algorithmically can be executed by a Turing Machine.

Conclusion

While von Neumann and Turing operated in different spheres of theoretical inquiry, their collaboration—however informal—was instrumental in shaping the field of computer science. Their ideas not only advanced the understanding of computation and algorithms but also inspired future generations of researchers and practitioners. The legacy of their work continues to resonate in contemporary discussions about artificial intelligence, machine learning, and the ethical implications of computing technologies.

In summary, the collaboration between John von Neumann and Alan Turing exemplifies the power of interdisciplinary dialogue in advancing scientific knowledge. Their combined efforts in theoretical computation and decision-making have left an indelible mark on the landscape of technology, ensuring that their contributions will not be forgotten in the annals of history.

Building the First Electronic Computer

The journey towards the creation of the first electronic computer is a tale woven with ambition, intellect, and a touch of serendipity. John von Neumann, alongside a cadre of brilliant minds, played a pivotal role in this groundbreaking endeavor during the early 1940s. This section delves into the conceptualization and realization of what would become the Electronic Numerical Integrator and Computer (ENIAC), a monumental leap in computational technology.

The Context of Computer Development

Before the advent of electronic computers, mechanical calculators and electromechanical devices dominated the landscape of computation. These machines, while innovative for their time, were limited in speed and efficiency. The need for a faster and more reliable computing device became increasingly apparent, especially during World War II, where complex calculations for artillery trajectories and cryptography were paramount.

Theoretical Foundations

At the heart of this revolution was the need for a new computational model. Von Neumann's insights into the architecture of computers led to the formulation of what is now known as the von Neumann architecture. This architecture is characterized by a stored-program concept, where both data and instructions are stored in the same memory space. This design contrasts sharply with earlier machines, which required separate storage for instructions and data, leading to inefficiencies.

The von Neumann architecture can be succinctly described with the following components:

- **Central Processing Unit (CPU)**: The brain of the computer, responsible for executing instructions.

- **Memory**: A storage area that holds both data and instructions.

- **Input/Output Devices**: Interfaces that allow communication between the computer and the outside world.

- **Bus System**: A communication system that transfers data between components.

Mathematically, the operations of the CPU can be defined using a simple instruction cycle:

$$\text{Instruction Cycle} = \text{Fetch} + \text{Decode} + \text{Execute} \tag{14}$$

Where: - *Fetch* involves retrieving the instruction from memory. - *Decode* translates the instruction into a form that can be executed. - *Execute* performs the operation specified by the instruction.

The ENIAC Project

The ENIAC project was initiated in 1943 at the University of Pennsylvania. Von Neumann, along with engineers like J. Presper Eckert and John Mauchly, laid the groundwork for this monumental machine. The original design was intended to solve complex differential equations, a task that would take conventional methods an impractical amount of time.

ENIAC's construction began in 1944, and it was officially completed in 1945. The machine comprised approximately 18,000 vacuum tubes, which served as the primary electronic switches. This choice of technology was revolutionary but also presented significant challenges, including heat generation and reliability issues.

The Challenges of Vacuum Tubes

The use of vacuum tubes was a double-edged sword. On one hand, they allowed for rapid switching and amplification of electrical signals, essential for high-speed calculations. On the other hand, they were prone to failure. The lifespan of a vacuum tube was limited, and the ENIAC would often require maintenance due to tube burnout.

The operational challenges were compounded by the complexity of programming the machine. Initially, the ENIAC was programmed using a series of plugboards and switches, a process that was labor-intensive and time-consuming. This led to the development of more sophisticated programming techniques, including the use of punched cards, which allowed for more efficient input of instructions.

The First Calculation

The first successful calculation performed by ENIAC was a ballistic trajectory computation for the United States Army. This achievement marked a significant milestone in computing history, showcasing the potential of electronic computers to perform complex calculations at unprecedented speeds. The ENIAC could execute thousands of operations per second, a staggering feat compared to its mechanical predecessors.

Legacy and Impact

The impact of ENIAC extended far beyond its initial applications. It laid the groundwork for future developments in computer science and engineering. The concept of a programmable computer, as proposed by von Neumann, became the foundation for subsequent generations of computers.

Von Neumann's contributions to the design and functionality of ENIAC not only revolutionized computation but also set the stage for the development of modern computing systems. His vision of a stored-program computer has influenced countless innovations in technology, leading to the sophisticated devices we rely on today.

In conclusion, the building of the first electronic computer was not merely an engineering achievement; it was a profound leap into the future of technology. John von Neumann's role in this endeavor exemplifies the intersection of theoretical mathematics and practical engineering, a hallmark of his enduring legacy in the realm of computer science.

The Father of Artificial Intelligence

Early Experiments in AI

The Logic Theorist Project

The Logic Theorist, often hailed as the first artificial intelligence program, was developed in 1955 by Allen Newell and Herbert A. Simon, with significant contributions from John von Neumann's foundational theories in logic and computation. This groundbreaking project aimed to explore the capabilities of machines to perform tasks that were traditionally considered exclusive to human intelligence: proving mathematical theorems.

Background and Objectives

The primary objective of the Logic Theorist was to simulate the problem-solving skills of a human mathematician. The program was designed to demonstrate that a computer could not only manipulate symbols but also understand logical relationships and derive conclusions from axioms. This marked a significant departure from previous computational tasks, which were largely arithmetic in nature.

Theoretical Foundations

The Logic Theorist was based on formal logic, particularly the principles of propositional calculus. At its core, the program utilized a method known as *heuristic search*, which allowed it to explore the space of possible proofs systematically. The key components of the program included:

- **Axioms and Theorems:** The program operated on a set of axioms, which are the foundational statements accepted as true without proof. For example, in propositional logic, one of the axioms could be:

$$A \implies (B \implies A)$$

- **Inference Rules:** The Logic Theorist employed inference rules to derive new theorems from existing ones. One of the most notable rules was Modus Ponens, which states:

$$\text{If } P \implies Q \text{ and } P \text{ is true, then } Q \text{ is true.}$$

Algorithmic Approach

The Logic Theorist utilized a search algorithm that could traverse the space of possible proofs. The algorithm could be summarized in the following steps:
1. **Initialization:** Load the axioms and the theorem to be proved. 2. **Search:** Systematically apply inference rules to generate new theorems. 3. **Goal Test:** Check if the generated theorem matches the target theorem. 4. **Backtrack:** If the current path does not lead to a solution, backtrack and try alternative paths.

This approach allowed the Logic Theorist to effectively navigate the complexities of mathematical proofs, mimicking the cognitive processes of human mathematicians.

Significant Achievements

The Logic Theorist achieved notable success in proving several theorems from *Principia Mathematica*, a seminal work by Alfred North Whitehead and Bertrand Russell. Among the most celebrated proofs was the demonstration of the following theorem:

$$\text{If } A \implies B \text{ and } B \implies C, \text{ then } A \implies C.$$

This theorem, known as the *Transitive Property*, was a landmark achievement in the realm of automated theorem proving.

Influence on Artificial Intelligence Research

The Logic Theorist laid the groundwork for future developments in artificial intelligence and cognitive science. It introduced the concept of heuristic search, which has since become a cornerstone in AI problem-solving strategies. The program demonstrated that machines could not only process information but could also engage in reasoning, a concept that would be pivotal in subsequent AI research.

Moreover, the success of the Logic Theorist prompted further exploration into other areas of AI, including natural language processing and machine learning. The principles established by Newell, Simon, and von Neumann in this project continue to influence the design of modern AI systems.

Conclusion

The Logic Theorist Project was a monumental step forward in the field of artificial intelligence. By proving that machines could replicate human-like reasoning, it opened the door to a new era of computational thinking. John von Neumann's contributions to the theoretical underpinnings of this project were crucial, as they provided the necessary framework for understanding the logical structures that govern mathematical reasoning. As we reflect on the legacy of the Logic Theorist, we recognize it not only as a pioneering program but also as a catalyst for the evolution of intelligent machines.

Theories on Machine Learning

Machine learning, a subfield of artificial intelligence, revolves around the idea that systems can learn from data, identify patterns, and make decisions with minimal human intervention. John von Neumann's contributions laid a foundational understanding that would later influence the development of machine learning theories.

Foundational Concepts in Machine Learning

At its core, machine learning involves algorithms that improve their performance on a task through experience. The primary components of machine learning can be summarized as follows:

- **Data:** The raw material from which models learn. Data can be labeled (supervised learning) or unlabeled (unsupervised learning).

- **Model:** A mathematical representation of the process generating the data. Models can take various forms, including decision trees, neural networks, and support vector machines.

- **Learning Algorithm:** The method used to update the model based on the data. This involves optimization techniques to minimize error.

- **Prediction:** The outcome generated by the model when new data is introduced.

Types of Learning

Machine learning can be broadly categorized into three types:

1. **Supervised Learning:** In supervised learning, models are trained on labeled datasets. The objective is to learn a mapping from inputs X to outputs Y. The relationship is often expressed as:

$$Y = f(X) + \epsilon$$

   where f represents the underlying function, and ϵ is the error term. A common algorithm used is linear regression, which minimizes the mean squared error:

$$\text{MSE} = \frac{1}{n} \sum_{i=1}^{n} (y_i - \hat{y}_i)^2$$

   where y_i is the true value and $\hat{y}_i$ is the predicted value.

2. **Unsupervised Learning:** In this approach, the model learns patterns from unlabeled data. Clustering is a popular unsupervised learning technique, with the K-means algorithm being a classic example. The algorithm seeks to partition n observations into k clusters by minimizing the within-cluster sum of squares:

$$J = \sum_{j=1}^{k} \sum_{i=1}^{n_j} \|x_i - \mu_j\|^2$$

   where n_j is the number of points in cluster j and μ_j is the centroid of cluster j.

3. **Reinforcement Learning:** This type of learning is based on the idea of agents taking actions in an environment to maximize cumulative rewards. The agent learns a policy π that maps states S to actions A to maximize the expected return R:

$$R = \sum_{t=0}^{\infty} \gamma^t r_t$$

   where r_t is the reward at time t and γ is the discount factor.

EARLY EXPERIMENTS IN AI

Key Theoretical Contributions

Von Neumann's influence on machine learning can be traced through several key theories:

Game Theory and Learning: John von Neumann was a pioneer in game theory, which has direct implications for machine learning, especially in multi-agent systems. The Nash equilibrium, a concept developed by John Nash, is critical in understanding how agents can optimize their strategies in competitive environments. The equilibrium can be represented as:

$$\pi_i^* = \arg\max_{\pi_i} E[u_i(\pi_i, \pi_{-i})]$$

where u_i is the utility function for player i and π_{-i} represents the strategies of other players.

The Perceptron Model: One of the earliest models of neural networks, the perceptron, aligns with von Neumann's vision of machine learning. The perceptron algorithm updates weights based on the error in predictions, defined as:

$$w \leftarrow w + \eta(y - \hat{y})x$$

where η is the learning rate, y is the true label, $\hat{y}$ is the predicted label, and x is the input feature vector.

Challenges in Machine Learning

Despite its advancements, machine learning faces several challenges that researchers continue to address:

- **Overfitting:** A model may perform well on training data but poorly on unseen data. Techniques such as regularization and cross-validation are employed to mitigate overfitting.

- **Bias-Variance Tradeoff:** Striking a balance between bias (error due to overly simplistic assumptions) and variance (error due to excessive complexity) is crucial for model performance.

- **Interpretability:** Many machine learning models, particularly deep learning models, are often viewed as "black boxes." Understanding how these models arrive at decisions remains an active area of research.

Conclusion

John von Neumann's legacy in the realm of machine learning is profound, providing a theoretical framework that continues to evolve. His interdisciplinary approach, which combined mathematics, computer science, and game theory, has paved the way for future innovations in artificial intelligence. As machine learning continues to advance, revisiting von Neumann's contributions will be essential in addressing the challenges and expanding the horizons of this dynamic field.

Influence on Future AI Research

John von Neumann's pioneering work in artificial intelligence (AI) laid the groundwork for many concepts and methodologies that continue to shape the field today. His early experiments and theoretical contributions provided a framework that researchers have built upon, leading to significant advancements in AI. In this section, we explore the key influences of von Neumann's work on future AI research, highlighting specific theories, problems, and examples that illustrate his lasting impact.

1. The Logic Theorist Project

One of von Neumann's notable contributions to AI was his involvement in the Logic Theorist project, which was developed by Allen Newell and Herbert A. Simon in the 1950s. This project aimed to create a program capable of proving mathematical theorems, effectively demonstrating the potential of machines to perform tasks traditionally reserved for human intellect. The Logic Theorist utilized a method called heuristic search, a technique that would become fundamental in AI problem-solving.

The success of the Logic Theorist was rooted in its ability to mimic human reasoning processes. Von Neumann's insights into formal logic and mathematical proof systems were instrumental in shaping the algorithms used in the project. The program was able to prove 38 of the first 52 theorems in Whitehead and Russell's "Principia Mathematica," showcasing the potential of AI to tackle complex logical problems.

2. Game Theory and Decision Making

Von Neumann's contributions to game theory also have profound implications for AI research. His formulation of the minimax theorem and the concept of Nash equilibrium have influenced AI algorithms, particularly in areas such as strategic decision-making and multi-agent systems. Game theory provides a mathematical framework for understanding competitive situations, allowing AI systems to make optimal decisions based on the actions of other agents.

The application of game theory in AI can be seen in various domains, including economics, robotics, and cybersecurity. For example, in multi-agent reinforcement learning, agents must learn to adapt their strategies based on the actions of their opponents. The principles established by von Neumann enable AI systems to evaluate potential outcomes and make informed decisions, ultimately enhancing their performance in competitive environments.

3. Machine Learning and Neural Networks

Von Neumann's work laid the foundation for the development of machine learning algorithms and neural networks. His exploration of automata theory and self-replicating machines inspired researchers to consider how machines could learn from data and improve their performance over time. The concept of a neural network, which is modeled after the human brain, draws on von Neumann's ideas about information processing and computation.

In particular, von Neumann's architecture, which separates memory and processing units, is reflected in modern neural network designs. The ability of neural networks to learn complex patterns and make predictions based on input data can be traced back to the theoretical principles established by von Neumann. For instance, convolutional neural networks (CNNs) have revolutionized image recognition tasks by leveraging hierarchical feature extraction, a concept that aligns with von Neumann's emphasis on structured information processing.

4. The Turing Test and Human-Like Intelligence

Von Neumann's collaboration with Alan Turing further advanced the discourse on machine intelligence. The Turing Test, proposed by Turing, evaluates a machine's ability to exhibit intelligent behavior indistinguishable from that of a human. Von Neumann's insights into computational theory and cognitive processes contributed to the development of benchmarks for assessing machine intelligence.

Future AI research continues to grapple with the challenges posed by the Turing Test. While significant progress has been made in natural language processing and conversational agents, achieving true human-like intelligence remains an elusive goal. Von Neumann's work encourages researchers to explore the complexities of cognition, perception, and reasoning, pushing the boundaries of what machines can achieve.

5. Ethical Considerations and AI Safety

As AI technology advances, von Neumann's foresight regarding the ethical implications of intelligent machines has become increasingly relevant. His involvement in the Manhattan Project and subsequent reflections on the moral responsibilities of scientists underscore the importance of considering the societal impact of AI. Future AI research must address ethical dilemmas, including bias in algorithms, accountability, and the potential for autonomous systems to make life-and-death decisions.

The establishment of ethical guidelines and safety protocols in AI development can be traced back to von Neumann's emphasis on responsible innovation. Researchers are now exploring frameworks for ensuring that AI systems align with human values and operate safely within societal norms. This ongoing dialogue reflects von Neumann's legacy as a thinker who recognized the profound implications of his work.

Conclusion

In summary, John von Neumann's influence on future AI research is profound and multifaceted. His contributions to logic, game theory, machine learning, and ethical considerations have shaped the trajectory of AI development. As researchers continue to explore the frontiers of artificial intelligence, they draw upon the foundational principles established by von Neumann, ensuring that his legacy endures in the quest for intelligent machines. The challenges and opportunities presented by AI today echo von Neumann's vision of a future where machines augment human capabilities and transform our understanding of intelligence itself.

The Legacy of von Neumann's AI Work

John von Neumann's contributions to the field of artificial intelligence (AI) are foundational, marking the transition from theoretical concepts to practical applications that would shape the future of computing. His work in AI was characterized by a blend of mathematical rigor and visionary foresight, enabling subsequent generations of researchers to build upon his ideas.

At the heart of von Neumann's legacy in AI is his pioneering work on the Logic Theorist, developed in collaboration with Herbert Simon in the mid-1950s. Often regarded as the first AI program, the Logic Theorist was capable of proving mathematical theorems by mimicking human reasoning processes. The program utilized a set of axioms and rules of inference to derive conclusions, demonstrating that machines could perform tasks traditionally reserved for human intellect. This was a significant breakthrough, as it challenged the prevailing notion of what machines could achieve.

$$\text{Theorem Proving:} \quad T \vdash A \quad \text{if } A \text{ can be derived from } T \text{ using rules of inference.} \tag{15}$$

Von Neumann's insights into game theory also played a crucial role in the development of AI. His formulation of the minimax theorem provided a framework for decision-making in competitive environments, which is fundamental in AI applications such as robotics and strategic game-playing algorithms. The theorem states that in a zero-sum game, there exists a strategy that minimizes the maximum possible loss, allowing AI systems to make optimal choices even under uncertainty.

$$\text{Minimax Theorem:} \quad \min_{a \in A} \max_{b \in B} L(a, b) \leq \max_{b \in B} \min_{a \in A} L(a, b) \tag{16}$$

Moreover, von Neumann's work on self-replicating machines laid the groundwork for concepts in evolutionary algorithms and genetic programming. His theoretical model of self-replication illustrated how machines could autonomously reproduce, a concept that has profound implications for AI and robotics today. This idea resonates in modern AI research, where systems are designed to adapt and evolve based on their environment, mimicking biological processes.

$$\text{Self-Replication:} \quad M \to M' \quad \text{where } M' \text{ is a copy of } M. \tag{17}$$

In addition to these theoretical contributions, von Neumann's interdisciplinary approach fostered collaboration across fields, influencing the trajectory of AI research. His interactions with contemporaries like Alan Turing and Norbert Wiener helped to shape a collective understanding of machine intelligence and its potential applications. This collaborative spirit is echoed in the modern AI community, which thrives on cross-disciplinary partnerships.

Von Neumann's legacy is also evident in the ethical considerations he raised regarding AI. His awareness of the potential consequences of autonomous systems foreshadowed contemporary debates on AI safety, ethics, and governance. He understood that as machines became more capable, the implications of their decisions would extend beyond mere calculations, impacting society at large. This foresight has become increasingly relevant in today's discussions on AI ethics, where the need for responsible AI development is paramount.

In summary, the legacy of John von Neumann's work in artificial intelligence is multifaceted and enduring. His pioneering efforts laid the groundwork for the field, influencing both the theoretical and practical aspects of AI. From theorem proving to self-replicating machines, von Neumann's contributions continue to resonate in contemporary research, inspiring new generations of innovators to explore the vast potential of artificial intelligence. His vision and intellectual rigor remain a guiding light in the ongoing quest to understand and harness the power of intelligent machines.

Controversies Surrounding von Neumann's AI Contributions

John von Neumann's contributions to the field of artificial intelligence (AI) were groundbreaking, yet they were not without their controversies. While he is often celebrated as a pioneer, his theories and experiments generated significant debate among contemporaries and later scholars. This section delves into the contentious aspects of von Neumann's work in AI, exploring the nuances of his theories, the challenges they presented, and the criticisms they faced.

The Dual Nature of von Neumann's Theories

One of the primary controversies surrounding von Neumann's AI contributions stems from the dual nature of his theoretical frameworks. On one hand, he introduced concepts that laid the groundwork for modern AI, such as the Logic Theorist, which was one of the first programs designed to mimic human problem-solving. This program demonstrated that machines could prove mathematical theorems, a groundbreaking assertion at the time.

However, critics argued that von Neumann's approach was overly optimistic. They contended that his work did not adequately address the complexities of human cognition. For instance, while von Neumann focused on formal logic and computational efficiency, many felt that this perspective neglected the emotional and contextual aspects of human reasoning. The contention here lies in the belief that AI, to truly replicate human intelligence, must also encompass these softer elements, an area where von Neumann's work was perceived as lacking.

The Ethics of Machine Learning

Another significant point of contention relates to the ethical implications of von Neumann's theories on machine learning. In his exploration of self-replicating machines, von Neumann hinted at the potential for machines to evolve independently of human control. This notion raised alarms among ethicists and philosophers, who questioned the moral ramifications of creating autonomous systems capable of self-improvement.

The ethical debate intensified with von Neumann's involvement in the development of the Manhattan Project and his advocacy for the use of computing in military applications. Critics argued that his contributions to AI could lead to the creation of autonomous weapons systems, sparking fears of a future where machines could make life-and-death decisions without human intervention. This concern remains relevant today, as discussions around AI ethics continue to evolve.

The Question of Originality

Von Neumann's contributions to AI also faced scrutiny regarding their originality. Some scholars have pointed out that while he was undoubtedly a brilliant mathematician, many of his ideas were built upon the work of earlier thinkers. For example, his theories on automata were influenced by the work of Alan Turing, who had already established foundational concepts in computation and intelligence.

This raises questions about the attribution of credit in the field of AI. Was von Neumann a true innovator, or was he merely synthesizing existing ideas? This debate has implications for how we understand the history of AI and the contributions of various individuals within it.

The Legacy of Controversy

Despite these controversies, von Neumann's work in AI has had a lasting impact. His theories continue to influence contemporary research, albeit with a more nuanced understanding of their limitations. For example, the concept of neural networks, which has gained prominence in modern AI, diverges significantly from von Neumann's original frameworks, incorporating insights from psychology and cognitive science.

Moreover, the controversies surrounding von Neumann's contributions have spurred further research and debate in the field of AI ethics. As scholars grapple with the implications of machine learning and autonomous systems, the questions raised by von Neumann's work remain relevant. His legacy serves as a reminder of the importance of interdisciplinary dialogue in the pursuit of technological advancement.

In conclusion, while John von Neumann's contributions to artificial intelligence were undeniably significant, they were also fraught with controversy. The debates surrounding his theories reflect broader tensions within the field, as scholars strive to balance the potential of AI with the ethical and philosophical questions it raises. As we continue to explore the frontiers of artificial intelligence, von Neumann's work remains a critical point of reference, illuminating both the possibilities and pitfalls of this rapidly evolving discipline.

$$\text{Logic Theorist}(P) \Rightarrow \text{Proof}(T) \tag{18}$$

In this equation, P represents the set of propositions, and T denotes the theorem being proved, encapsulating the essence of von Neumann's approach to AI through formal logic.

$$\text{AI}_{\text{Ethics}} = f(\text{Autonomy, Control, Responsibility}) \tag{19}$$

Here, $\text{AI}_{\text{Ethics}}$ is a function that represents the ethical considerations in AI, influenced by factors such as autonomy, control, and responsibility—elements that were crucial in the controversies surrounding von Neumann's contributions.

Through these discussions, we can appreciate the complexity of von Neumann's legacy in AI, acknowledging both his pioneering efforts and the critical conversations they have inspired.

Beyond Computer Science: Interdisciplinary Innovations

Contributions to Physics

The von Neumann Entropy Theory

In the realm of quantum mechanics, the concept of entropy plays a crucial role in understanding the behavior of physical systems. John von Neumann, a towering figure in mathematics and physics, made significant contributions to this field through his formulation of quantum entropy, which is an extension of the classical notion of entropy to quantum systems. This section delves into the foundations of von Neumann entropy, its mathematical formulation, and its implications in quantum mechanics.

Definition of von Neumann Entropy

The von Neumann entropy, denoted as $S(\rho)$, is defined for a quantum state represented by the density matrix ρ. The mathematical expression for von Neumann entropy is given by:

$$S(\rho) = -\text{Tr}(\rho \log \rho) \qquad (20)$$

where Tr denotes the trace operation, which sums the diagonal elements of the matrix, and log is the logarithm to the base 2. The density matrix ρ encapsulates all the statistical information about a quantum system, and its eigenvalues correspond to the probabilities of the system being in various quantum states.

Properties of von Neumann Entropy

Von Neumann entropy possesses several important properties that mirror those of classical entropy:

- **Non-negativity:** The entropy is always non-negative, $S(\rho) \geq 0$. This is a consequence of the fact that the eigenvalues of ρ are non-negative.

- **Zero Entropy:** The entropy is zero if and only if the system is in a pure state. For a pure state represented by a density matrix $\rho = |\psi\rangle\langle\psi|$, we have:

$$S(\rho) = 0. \tag{21}$$

- **Additivity:** For two independent quantum systems described by density matrices ρ_A and ρ_B, the entropy of the combined system is the sum of the entropies:

$$S(\rho_{AB}) = S(\rho_A) + S(\rho_B). \tag{22}$$

Example: Calculating von Neumann Entropy

To illustrate the calculation of von Neumann entropy, consider a simple quantum system with a density matrix given by:

$$\rho = \begin{pmatrix} 0.8 & 0 \\ 0 & 0.2 \end{pmatrix}$$

This matrix describes a mixed state with probabilities $p_1 = 0.8$ and $p_2 = 0.2$ for two orthogonal states. The eigenvalues of this density matrix are $\lambda_1 = 0.8$ and $\lambda_2 = 0.2$.

Using the definition of von Neumann entropy, we compute:

$$\begin{aligned} S(\rho) &= -\mathrm{Tr}(\rho \log \rho) \\ &= -(0.8 \log(0.8) + 0.2 \log(0.2)). \end{aligned}$$

Calculating the logarithms (using base 2):

$$\begin{aligned} \log(0.8) &\approx -0.32193, \\ \log(0.2) &\approx -2.32193. \end{aligned}$$

Substituting these values back into the entropy formula:

$$S(\rho)\& = -\,(0.8 \cdot (-0.32193) + 0.2 \cdot (-2.32193))$$
$$\& = 0.8 \cdot 0.32193 + 0.2 \cdot 2.32193$$
$$\& \approx 0.257544 + 0.464386 = 0.72193.$$

Thus, the von Neumann entropy of the given state is approximately $S(\rho) \approx 0.72193$.

Applications of von Neumann Entropy

The concept of von Neumann entropy is not merely a theoretical construct; it has profound implications in various domains of quantum physics and information theory. Some notable applications include:

- **Quantum Information Theory:** Von Neumann entropy serves as a measure of the information content of a quantum state. It is instrumental in quantifying the amount of information that can be extracted from a quantum system.

- **Quantum Thermodynamics:** In the context of quantum thermodynamics, von Neumann entropy is used to describe the thermodynamic properties of quantum systems, allowing for the exploration of concepts such as temperature and heat exchange in quantum contexts.

- **Quantum Computing:** The efficiency of quantum algorithms can be analyzed using von Neumann entropy, particularly in understanding the entanglement and coherence of quantum states.

Conclusion

John von Neumann's formulation of entropy in quantum mechanics has left an indelible mark on the field. The von Neumann entropy theory not only extends classical concepts of entropy into the quantum realm but also provides a powerful tool for analyzing and understanding quantum systems. As quantum technologies continue to evolve, the relevance of von Neumann's insights will undoubtedly persist, inspiring future generations of physicists and computer scientists to explore the depths of quantum information and its myriad applications.

Quantum Computing and von Neumann Algebras

Quantum computing represents a paradigm shift in computational theory and practice, leveraging the principles of quantum mechanics to process information in fundamentally different ways compared to classical computing. At the heart of this revolutionary field lies the mathematical framework of von Neumann algebras, which provides a robust structure for understanding quantum systems and their operations.

The Basics of Quantum Computing

Quantum bits, or qubits, are the fundamental units of quantum information. Unlike classical bits that can exist in one of two states (0 or 1), qubits can exist in a superposition of states, represented mathematically as:

$$|\psi\rangle = \alpha|0\rangle + \beta|1\rangle$$

where $|\alpha|^2 + |\beta|^2 = 1$. This property allows quantum computers to perform many calculations simultaneously, leading to an exponential increase in computational power for certain problems.

Von Neumann Algebras: A Brief Overview

The concept of von Neumann algebras, introduced by John von Neumann in the 1930s, is pivotal in the mathematical foundation of quantum mechanics. A von Neumann algebra is a *-subalgebra of bounded operators on a Hilbert space that is closed under the weak operator topology. This closure property is crucial for ensuring that quantum measurements and their associated probabilities are well-defined.

Formally, a von Neumann algebra $\mathcal{M}$ can be defined as follows:

$$\mathcal{M} \subseteq B(H)$$

where $B(H)$ denotes the bounded linear operators on a Hilbert space H. The key properties of von Neumann algebras include:

- **Self-adjointness:** If $A \in \mathcal{M}$, then $A^* \in \mathcal{M}$. - **Closure:** If $A_n \in \mathcal{M}$ and $A_n \to A$ in the weak operator topology, then $A \in \mathcal{M}$.

Quantum Measurements and Observables

In quantum mechanics, observables are represented by self-adjoint operators on a Hilbert space. The spectral theorem allows us to express any self-adjoint operator A in terms of its eigenvalues and eigenvectors:

$$A = \sum_i \lambda_i P_i$$

where λ_i are the eigenvalues and P_i are the corresponding projection operators. The projections P_i belong to a von Neumann algebra, encapsulating the measurement process and the probabilistic nature of quantum mechanics.

Applications of Von Neumann Algebras in Quantum Computing

Von Neumann algebras find numerous applications in quantum computing, particularly in the study of quantum error correction, quantum information theory, and the formulation of quantum algorithms. One prominent application is in the development of quantum error-correcting codes, which are essential for protecting quantum information from decoherence and operational errors.

Quantum Error Correction Quantum error correction exploits the structure of von Neumann algebras to encode quantum information in a way that allows for the recovery of information even when some qubits are corrupted. The main idea is to use multiple physical qubits to represent a single logical qubit, thereby creating redundancy that can be exploited to detect and correct errors.

A classic example is the Shor code, which encodes a single logical qubit into nine physical qubits. The logical state $|\psi_L\rangle$ can be expressed as:

$$|\psi_L\rangle = \frac{1}{2}(|000\rangle + |111\rangle) \otimes (|000\rangle + |111\rangle) \otimes (|000\rangle + |111\rangle)$$

This redundancy ensures that even if one or two qubits are flipped due to noise, the logical information can still be recovered.

The Future of Quantum Computing and von Neumann Algebras

As quantum computing continues to evolve, the role of von Neumann algebras will likely expand, particularly in the realms of quantum algorithms and quantum cryptography. Researchers are exploring new quantum algorithms that leverage the mathematical properties of these algebras to enhance computational efficiency and security.

Furthermore, the study of non-commutative geometry, which extends von Neumann algebra theory, may lead to novel insights into quantum gravity and the fundamental nature of spacetime, bridging the gap between quantum mechanics and general relativity.

In conclusion, the interplay between quantum computing and von Neumann algebras exemplifies the depth and complexity of modern computational theory. As we delve deeper into this fascinating intersection, we uncover not only the potential for unprecedented computational power but also the profound philosophical implications of a quantum world governed by the elegant mathematics of von Neumann.

Collaboration with Richard Feynman

John von Neumann and Richard Feynman, two titans of 20th-century science, found themselves at the intersection of physics and mathematics, where their collaborative efforts would yield profound insights into the nature of quantum mechanics and computation. Their work exemplified the merging of theoretical principles with practical applications, setting the stage for advancements that would resonate through the decades.

The Quantum Mechanical Framework

At the heart of their collaboration lay the burgeoning field of quantum mechanics, a domain that challenged classical intuitions and required innovative mathematical formulations. Von Neumann's seminal work, *Mathematical Foundations of Quantum Mechanics*, published in 1932, introduced the concept of Hilbert spaces and operators, providing a rigorous mathematical framework for quantum theory. He formulated the state of a quantum system as a vector in a complex vector space, where observable quantities correspond to self-adjoint operators.

The mathematical formulation can be expressed as follows:

$$\hat{A}\psi = a\psi \qquad (23)$$

where $\hat{A}$ is the operator representing an observable, ψ is the state vector (wave function), and a represents the eigenvalue corresponding to the measurement outcome.

Feynman, known for his intuitive grasp of quantum mechanics, contributed significantly to the interpretation and application of these principles. His path integral formulation of quantum mechanics, introduced in the 1940s, offered an alternative perspective that emphasized the sum over histories, enabling a profound understanding of particle behavior.

Von Neumann Algebras and Quantum Statistical Mechanics

The collaboration between von Neumann and Feynman extended into the realm of quantum statistical mechanics. Von Neumann's work on von Neumann algebras provided a foundation for understanding the mathematical structures underlying quantum measurements and the evolution of quantum states. He established the concept of *density operators*, which describe statistical mixtures of quantum states:

$$\rho = \sum_i p_i |\psi_i\rangle\langle\psi_i| \tag{24}$$

where ρ is the density operator, p_i are the probabilities of the states $|\psi_i\rangle$, and the sum runs over all possible states.

Feynman's insights into quantum field theory complemented von Neumann's algebraic approach, allowing for a more comprehensive understanding of particle interactions. Their discussions often revolved around the implications of quantum entanglement and the measurement problem, which would later become central themes in the philosophy of quantum mechanics.

Computational Techniques in Quantum Physics

A significant aspect of their collaboration involved the development of computational techniques for solving complex quantum mechanical problems. Feynman famously proposed that quantum systems could be simulated using other quantum systems, laying the groundwork for the concept of quantum computing. He recognized that classical computers faced inherent limitations when simulating quantum phenomena, leading him to suggest that a quantum computer could efficiently perform calculations that were infeasible for classical machines.

Von Neumann's contributions to the architecture of electronic computers, particularly the von Neumann architecture, provided a blueprint for future developments in computing. This architecture, characterized by a stored-program concept, allowed for the manipulation of data and instructions within a single framework. The fundamental structure can be represented as:

$$\text{Memory} \leftrightarrow \text{CPU} \leftrightarrow \text{I/O Devices} \tag{25}$$

where the central processing unit (CPU) executes instructions stored in memory, interacting with input and output devices to perform computations.

Legacy of Their Collaboration

The collaboration between von Neumann and Feynman was not merely an academic partnership; it was a confluence of ideas that reshaped the landscape of modern physics and computation. Their innovative approaches to quantum mechanics and computation laid the groundwork for the development of quantum information theory, a field that has gained prominence in recent years with the advent of quantum computing technologies.

The legacy of their collaboration can be seen in the ongoing research into quantum algorithms, quantum cryptography, and the quest for a unified theory of quantum gravity. Von Neumann's mathematical rigor combined with Feynman's intuitive insights created a synergy that continues to inspire physicists and computer scientists alike.

In conclusion, the collaboration between John von Neumann and Richard Feynman marked a pivotal moment in the history of science. Their joint efforts not only advanced the understanding of quantum mechanics but also paved the way for the future of computing, illustrating the profound impact of interdisciplinary collaboration in the pursuit of knowledge.

Impact on Modern Physics

John von Neumann's contributions to modern physics are as profound as they are multifaceted, spanning various domains from quantum mechanics to statistical mechanics. His work laid foundational principles that continue to influence contemporary physics, demonstrating the interplay between mathematics and physical theory.

Quantum Mechanics and von Neumann Algebras

One of von Neumann's most significant contributions to physics is his development of the mathematical framework known as *von Neumann algebras*. This framework emerged from his seminal work in quantum mechanics, specifically in the formulation of quantum theory in a rigorous mathematical context.

In his 1932 book, *Mathematical Foundations of Quantum Mechanics*, von Neumann introduced the concept of a *Hilbert space* as the mathematical setting for quantum states. A Hilbert space is a complete vector space equipped with an inner product, allowing for the representation of quantum states as vectors. The operators acting on these states, particularly self-adjoint operators, represent observable quantities.

The von Neumann algebra, a special type of operator algebra, arises when considering sets of bounded operators on a Hilbert space that are closed under the operator norm. This concept is crucial for understanding the structure of quantum mechanics, as it allows for the formulation of quantum observables and their associated measurement processes.

The mathematical formalism can be expressed as follows:

$$\mathcal{M} \subseteq B(\mathcal{H})$$

where $\mathcal{M}$ is the von Neumann algebra and $B(\mathcal{H})$ denotes the bounded linear operators on the Hilbert space $\mathcal{H}$.

Statistical Mechanics and Entropy

Von Neumann also made significant strides in statistical mechanics, particularly through his formulation of the concept of *entropy*. His work on entropy is encapsulated in the *von Neumann entropy*, defined for a quantum state described by a density operator ρ:

$$S(\rho) = -\text{Tr}(\rho \log \rho)$$

This equation captures the degree of uncertainty or disorder in a quantum system, analogous to classical thermodynamic entropy. Von Neumann's formulation not only provided a bridge between quantum mechanics and statistical mechanics but also paved the way for deeper insights into the nature of information in physical systems.

The von Neumann entropy has implications for various fields, including quantum information theory, where it serves as a measure of entanglement and information content. The relationship between entropy and information can be succinctly expressed as:

$$I = S(\rho_A) + S(\rho_B) - S(\rho_{AB})$$

where I represents the mutual information between two subsystems A and B, and ρ_{AB} is the joint density operator of the combined system.

Collaboration with Richard Feynman

Von Neumann's influence extended through his collaborations with other prominent physicists, notably Richard Feynman. Their discussions on the foundations of quantum mechanics and computation led to the conceptualization of quantum computing—a field that has gained immense traction in recent years.

Feynman's work on quantum electrodynamics and his path integral formulation were deeply informed by von Neumann's mathematical rigor. Their collaborative spirit exemplified the synergy between theoretical physics and advanced mathematics, resulting in groundbreaking advancements in understanding particle interactions and quantum field theory.

The Legacy of von Neumann's Work

The impact of von Neumann's contributions is evident in numerous modern developments in physics. His mathematical formulations have become essential tools for physicists, influencing areas such as quantum field theory, condensed matter physics, and even cosmology.

For instance, the application of von Neumann's principles can be seen in the formulation of quantum statistical mechanics, where the behavior of many-body systems is analyzed through the lens of entropy and operator algebras. This approach has led to significant advancements in understanding phase transitions and critical phenomena.

Moreover, the principles of quantum mechanics, underpinned by von Neumann's work, have led to the development of technologies such as quantum computing and quantum cryptography, which promise to revolutionize information processing and security.

In conclusion, John von Neumann's impact on modern physics is profound and enduring. His rigorous mathematical approach and interdisciplinary collaborations have not only advanced theoretical physics but have also laid the groundwork for future innovations in technology and science. As we continue to explore the complexities of the universe, the legacy of von Neumann serves as a guiding light, illuminating the path forward in our quest for knowledge.

Speculations on von Neumann's Involvement in Classified Research

John von Neumann, a towering figure in the realms of mathematics, physics, and computer science, has long been shrouded in a veil of intrigue and speculation regarding his potential involvement in classified research. This section delves into

CONTRIBUTIONS TO PHYSICS

the theories and conjectures surrounding his activities during a pivotal era in history, particularly during and after World War II, when the boundaries between scientific inquiry and national security began to blur.

The Context of War and Innovation

The backdrop of World War II was a crucible for scientific innovation, with the Manhattan Project serving as a prime example of how urgent military needs can catalyze groundbreaking research. Von Neumann's early involvement in the project, particularly in the development of the atomic bomb, positioned him at the intersection of science and state secrecy. His expertise in hydrodynamics and shock waves was instrumental in understanding the implosion mechanism of nuclear weapons, leading to the successful detonation of the first atomic bomb in 1945.

Theoretical Contributions to Military Technology

Von Neumann's contributions were not limited to theoretical physics; they extended into the realm of game theory and operations research, both of which have profound implications for military strategy. His formulation of the minimax theorem, which provides a strategy for minimizing the possible loss in a worst-case scenario, became a foundational concept in military decision-making. The equation can be expressed as:

$$V = \max_{s \in S} \min_{t \in T} L(s, t) \tag{26}$$

where V represents the value of the strategy, S is the set of strategies available to the player, and T is the set of strategies available to the opponent. This strategic framework has been applied extensively in military contexts, leading to speculation about von Neumann's direct involvement in classified military operations.

Collaboration with Government Agencies

Post-war, von Neumann's relationship with the U.S. government deepened, particularly with the establishment of the Atomic Energy Commission (AEC) and the Defense Department. His role as a consultant and advisor in these agencies has led to conjectures about his participation in classified projects, including early research into thermonuclear weapons. Notably, von Neumann's work on the development of the hydrogen bomb, which involved complex calculations of thermonuclear reactions, was conducted under a shroud of secrecy.

The implications of his research in these areas are profound, as they not only advanced military technology but also raised ethical questions regarding the responsibilities of scientists in wartime. His famous quote, "The scientist is not a person who gives the right answers; he's one who asks the right questions," underscores the moral dilemmas faced by scientists like von Neumann who operated within a classified context.

Speculative Theories on Espionage and Intelligence

The intrigue surrounding von Neumann's classified work has also given rise to theories of espionage. Some historians speculate that his connections with various government agencies may have involved information sharing that went beyond conventional research. For example, his collaboration with figures in the intelligence community, such as General Leslie Groves, has led to questions about whether von Neumann was privy to classified information that could have influenced his academic work.

Moreover, von Neumann's interest in game theory has been linked to intelligence strategies during the Cold War. His concepts of zero-sum games and strategic dominance could have provided insights into the behavior of adversaries, leading to speculation that his work was utilized for espionage purposes. The mathematical formulations of these theories, including the Nash equilibrium, where players reach a state of mutual benefit, can be expressed as:

$$\text{If } (x_1, x_2, \ldots, x_n) \text{ is a Nash equilibrium, then } u_i(x_1, x_2, \ldots, x_n) \geq u_i(x_1, x_2, \ldots, x'_i, \ldots) \quad (27)$$

where u_i represents the utility function for player i, and x'_i represents a deviation from the equilibrium strategy.

Legacy of Secrecy and Speculation

The legacy of John von Neumann is one marked by his extraordinary contributions to science and technology. However, the speculative nature of his involvement in classified research adds a layer of complexity to his biography. The intersection of his mathematical genius with the demands of national security raises questions about the ethical implications of scientific research in wartime.

As we reexamine von Neumann's life and contributions, it is essential to recognize the duality of his legacy: a brilliant mind that propelled humanity into the future while simultaneously navigating the murky waters of secrecy and espionage. The unresolved questions about his classified work continue to intrigue historians and scholars, leaving us to ponder the true extent of his involvement in the shadowy realms of government research.

In conclusion, while definitive evidence of von Neumann's direct involvement in espionage remains elusive, the speculations surrounding his classified research highlight the intricate relationship between science, ethics, and national security. As we reflect on his contributions, we must also consider the broader implications of scientific inquiry in a world where knowledge can be both a tool for progress and a weapon of war.

The Unconventional Mind

Personal Life: Eccentricities and Relationships

von Neumann's Gaming Obsession

John von Neumann, a towering figure in the realms of mathematics, physics, and computer science, also had a lesser-known but equally fascinating passion: gaming. His obsession with games wasn't merely a pastime; it was a fundamental part of his intellectual pursuits and contributed significantly to his groundbreaking work in various fields, particularly in game theory.

The Intersection of Games and Mathematics

Von Neumann's interest in games can be traced back to his early life, where he exhibited prodigious talent in mathematics. He was known to play card games and chess, often employing mathematical strategies to outmaneuver his opponents. This fascination led him to formalize the study of strategic interactions, culminating in the development of game theory—a mathematical framework for analyzing competitive situations where the outcome depends on the actions of multiple agents.

Game Theory: The Mathematical Playground

Game theory, as pioneered by von Neumann, provides essential insights into decision-making processes in competitive environments. The fundamental components of game theory include players, strategies, payoffs, and information. One of the most significant contributions von Neumann made to this field is the formulation of the minimax theorem.

$$\text{minimax} = \max_{s \in S} \min_{t \in T} u(s, t) \tag{28}$$

In this equation, S represents the strategies available to one player, T the strategies available to the opponent, and $u(s, t)$ the utility or payoff function. The minimax theorem asserts that in zero-sum games, there exists a strategy for each player that minimizes their maximum possible loss, thus ensuring a stable outcome.

Practical Applications of Game Theory

Von Neumann's work on game theory was not merely theoretical; it found applications in economics, political science, and evolutionary biology. For example, the Nash equilibrium, developed later by John Nash, extends von Neumann's ideas and has become a cornerstone of modern economic theory. The concept of Nash equilibrium describes a situation where no player can benefit by changing their strategy while the other players keep theirs unchanged.

Games of Chance and Strategy

Von Neumann was particularly drawn to games that combined elements of chance and strategy, such as poker. He viewed poker not just as a game of luck but as a complex interplay of probability, psychology, and strategy. His approach to poker exemplified his analytical mindset, where he would calculate odds and assess the behavior of opponents to make informed decisions.

The Legacy of von Neumann's Gaming Obsession

Von Neumann's gaming obsession transcended mere enjoyment; it became a driving force behind his intellectual achievements. His ability to apply mathematical principles to games laid the groundwork for various fields, including economics and artificial intelligence. The strategic thinking he cultivated through gaming influenced his later work on the development of algorithms and computational models.

In summary, John von Neumann's gaming obsession was not an isolated quirk but a reflection of his genius. It shaped his contributions to game theory and provided a unique lens through which he viewed complex problems. His legacy continues to inspire researchers and practitioners across disciplines, reminding us that the pursuit of knowledge can often be found in the most unexpected places—like a game of cards or chess.

Conclusion

In conclusion, von Neumann's passion for gaming exemplifies how leisure activities can fuel intellectual innovation. By engaging with games, he not only found joy but also developed critical insights that would resonate throughout the fields of mathematics, economics, and beyond. His gaming obsession serves as a testament to the idea that play can be a powerful catalyst for creativity and discovery.

The Mathematician and Musician

John von Neumann, often celebrated for his groundbreaking contributions to mathematics and computer science, was also a passionate musician. His dual interests in mathematics and music reveal the interplay between these two disciplines and how they influenced his thinking and creativity. This section explores von Neumann's musical inclinations, his mathematical insights into music theory, and how these elements coalesced in his life and work.

The Intersection of Mathematics and Music

Mathematics and music share a deep and intrinsic relationship. At the heart of music lies rhythm, harmony, and structure, all of which can be described mathematically. The connection between the two can be seen through concepts such as frequency, ratios, and patterns. Von Neumann recognized these parallels and often drew upon his mathematical expertise to explore musical compositions.

Frequency and Pitch The foundation of musical notes is built upon frequencies. Each note corresponds to a specific frequency, and the relationship between these frequencies determines the harmony of musical pieces. For example, the note A4 (the A above middle C) has a frequency of 440 Hz. When two notes are played together, the ratio of their frequencies can create consonance or dissonance.

The mathematical relationship can be expressed as follows:

$$\text{Frequency Ratio} = \frac{f_1}{f_2}$$

where f_1 and f_2 are the frequencies of two notes. For instance, the octave relationship, where one note is double the frequency of another, can be represented as:

$$\frac{f_1}{f_2} = 2$$

This ratio produces a pleasing sound, which is why octaves are fundamental in music theory.

Mathematical Patterns in Music

Von Neumann was fascinated by the patterns that emerge in both mathematics and music. He often explored the concept of symmetry, which is prevalent in musical compositions. Symmetrical structures can be found in various forms, such as scales, chords, and motifs.

For example, consider the construction of a major scale, which can be represented by the following whole and half-step pattern:

$$W\text{-}W\text{-}H\text{-}W\text{-}W\text{-}W\text{-}H$$

where W represents a whole step and H represents a half step. This pattern creates a symmetrical structure that is foundational to Western music.

The Fibonacci Sequence and Music Another mathematical concept that von Neumann appreciated was the Fibonacci sequence. This sequence, defined recursively as:

$$F(n) = F(n-1) + F(n-2)$$

with initial conditions $F(0) = 0$ and $F(1) = 1$, results in a series of numbers where each number is the sum of the two preceding ones. The Fibonacci sequence appears in various natural phenomena and has been used in musical compositions to create patterns and structures.

For example, some composers have utilized the Fibonacci sequence to determine the lengths of phrases in their works, leading to a natural, organic feel in the music. This connection between mathematics and music exemplifies von Neumann's belief in the beauty of mathematical relationships.

Von Neumann's Musical Pursuits

Von Neumann was an accomplished pianist and often played for friends and colleagues. His love for music was not merely a hobby; it was a significant part of his life. He believed that music provided a mental escape and fostered creativity, which complemented his rigorous mathematical work.

The Role of Music in Creative Thinking   Research has shown that engaging with music can enhance cognitive abilities and foster creative thinking. Von Neumann's ability to switch between mathematical rigor and musical expression exemplified this phenomenon. His musical pursuits likely contributed to his innovative thinking in mathematics and computer science.

Conclusion

In conclusion, John von Neumann's dual identity as a mathematician and musician illustrates the profound connections between these two fields. His understanding of mathematical principles enriched his musical experiences, while his musicality provided a creative outlet that complemented his scientific endeavors. The interplay between mathematics and music not only shaped von Neumann's life but also serves as a reminder of the beauty and harmony that can be found in the synthesis of seemingly disparate disciplines.

Extramarital Affairs and Open Relationships

John von Neumann, a mind that danced on the precipice of genius, was not just a titan of mathematics and computing; he was also a complex individual whose personal life reflected a tapestry of unconventional relationships. His extramarital affairs and open relationships provide a glimpse into the enigmatic personality that was von Neumann, illustrating the interplay between his intellectual pursuits and personal desires.

The Nature of Relationships

Von Neumann's relationships were characterized by a distinct lack of traditional boundaries. This was not merely a reflection of his personal preferences but also a manifestation of the era's evolving social norms. The mid-20th century saw a burgeoning acceptance of alternative relationship structures, particularly among intellectuals and artists. In this context, von Neumann's approach can be analyzed through the lens of *non-monogamous ethics*, which challenges the conventional paradigms of love, fidelity, and commitment.

Philosophical Underpinnings

The philosophical framework surrounding open relationships can be traced back to various ethical theories, including *utilitarianism* and *existentialism*. Utilitarianism posits that the best action is the one that maximizes overall happiness. In von

Neumann's case, his relationships may have been viewed as a means to enhance personal fulfillment and emotional satisfaction for himself and his partners. Conversely, existentialism emphasizes individual freedom and the creation of one's essence through choices. Von Neumann's choices in love and companionship reflected his desire to live authentically, free from societal constraints.

Examples of Relationships

One notable relationship involved his affair with *Margaret*, a fellow mathematician who shared his passion for intellectual discourse. Their relationship was marked by a mutual understanding of each other's commitments, both personal and professional. This dynamic exemplifies the principles of *polyamory*, where love is not limited to one partner but can be shared among multiple individuals.

In addition, von Neumann's marriage to *Klara* was characterized by a level of openness that was rare for the time. Klara, a supportive partner, often engaged with von Neumann's social circle, which included other intellectuals and scientists. This arrangement allowed for a unique blend of companionship and freedom, enabling both partners to explore their desires while maintaining a strong familial bond.

Theoretical Implications

The implications of von Neumann's relationship choices extend beyond personal anecdotes; they challenge traditional notions of loyalty and commitment. The *Game Theory* concepts he pioneered can be applied to analyze the strategic interactions within his relationships. For instance, consider the *Prisoner's Dilemma*, where two individuals must decide whether to cooperate or betray each other. In the context of open relationships, the dynamics shift as partners negotiate their desires, leading to a more complex interplay of trust and communication.

$$\text{Payoff} = \begin{cases} R & \text{if both cooperate} \\ T & \text{if one defects} \\ S & \text{if one cooperates and the other defects} \\ P & \text{if both defect} \end{cases} \qquad (29)$$

In this equation, R represents the reward for mutual cooperation (a harmonious open relationship), while T and S represent the outcomes of betrayal and cooperation, respectively. The challenge lies in establishing a framework where both partners can achieve the optimal payoff through honest communication and mutual respect.

Cultural Context

Culturally, von Neumann's relationships can be seen as a reflection of the societal shifts occurring during the post-war era. The rise of *free love* movements and the questioning of traditional marriage norms provided fertile ground for individuals like von Neumann to explore alternative lifestyles. This cultural backdrop allowed for a more liberated approach to love and companionship, one that resonated with von Neumann's own intellectual rebellion against conventional boundaries.

Conclusion

In conclusion, John von Neumann's extramarital affairs and open relationships offer a fascinating insight into the life of a man who defied categorization. His relationships were not merely personal escapades but a reflection of his broader philosophical beliefs about love, freedom, and the human experience. By examining these aspects of his life, we gain a deeper understanding of the complexities that shaped one of history's most brilliant minds. Von Neumann's legacy, therefore, extends beyond his contributions to mathematics and computing; it encompasses the very essence of what it means to be human in a world of infinite possibilities.

The enigmatic Personality of von Neumann

John von Neumann was not just a towering intellect in mathematics and computer science; he was also a complex and enigmatic individual whose personality defied easy categorization. His brilliance was often overshadowed by his peculiar habits and idiosyncrasies, making him a fascinating figure in the annals of scientific history.

The Dual Nature of Genius

At the core of von Neumann's enigmatic personality lay a duality that many geniuses possess: a brilliant mind coupled with a social awkwardness that made him both captivating and elusive. His ability to grasp complex mathematical concepts and derive profound insights was matched only by his struggle to relate to the mundane aspects of daily life. This duality is often encapsulated in the notion of *intellectual isolation*, where the pursuit of knowledge can lead to a disconnect from the broader human experience.

The Social Butterfly and the Solitary Thinker

Despite his reputation as a solitary thinker, von Neumann was known to be quite sociable, particularly in academic circles. He had a charming, charismatic presence that drew people to him, yet he often seemed to exist in a world of his own. His colleagues would describe him as a *social butterfly* at conferences and gatherings, engaging in lively discussions about mathematics and physics. However, those who ventured to know him on a deeper level often found him to be a *solitary thinker*, deeply engrossed in his thoughts and ideas, sometimes to the exclusion of those around him.

Eccentricities and Quirks

Von Neumann's eccentricities were legendary. He had a penchant for gambling, often engaging in high-stakes poker games where he would apply his mathematical prowess to gain an edge over his opponents. This obsession with games extended beyond cards; he was fascinated by strategy and probability, which ultimately led to his foundational work in game theory. His gambling habits were not just a pastime; they were a reflection of his desire to understand risk and decision-making, concepts he would later formalize in his academic work.

Moreover, he had a unique approach to problem-solving that involved a playful manipulation of ideas. For instance, he would often sketch diagrams and models on napkins during meetings, transforming abstract concepts into visual representations. This habit exemplified his ability to think outside the box, yet it also contributed to his enigmatic persona, as many struggled to follow his rapid-fire thought processes.

The Mathematician and the Musician

Another facet of von Neumann's personality was his deep appreciation for music. He was an accomplished pianist and often found solace in playing classical compositions. Music provided him with a creative outlet that complemented his analytical mind. This intersection of mathematics and music is not uncommon among great thinkers; both disciplines share a reliance on patterns, structures, and creativity.

In fact, von Neumann's understanding of musical theory influenced his mathematical work. He often drew parallels between musical composition and mathematical proofs, suggesting that both require a degree of artistic intuition. His ability to navigate these two worlds further illustrated the complexity of his character—he was not merely a mathematician; he was a creator, an artist in his own right.

Personal Relationships and Intriguities

Von Neumann's personal relationships were equally complex. He was known for his open relationships and extramarital affairs, which often raised eyebrows among his contemporaries. These aspects of his life revealed a man who was not bound by conventional norms, choosing instead to explore the depths of human connection in ways that were often unconventional.

His relationships were characterized by a blend of intellectual camaraderie and emotional detachment. He sought partners who could engage with him intellectually, yet he often struggled to form deeper emotional bonds. This paradoxical nature of his relationships contributed to the enigmatic aura that surrounded him—he was a man of intellect and passion, yet also one of emotional distance.

The Mysterious Final Days

As von Neumann's life drew to a close, his enigmatic personality took on a more poignant tone. Diagnosed with cancer in the early 1950s, he faced his illness with a stoicism that belied his inner turmoil. His final days were marked by a sense of urgency to impart his knowledge and insights to the next generation, yet he remained a figure shrouded in mystery, even in his vulnerability.

In his last public appearances, he continued to engage with colleagues and students, sharing his thoughts on the future of computing and artificial intelligence. However, the man who had once been a vibrant force in the scientific community now seemed to embody the very enigma that had defined his life—a brilliant mind grappling with the inevitability of mortality.

Conclusion

John von Neumann's enigmatic personality was a tapestry woven from threads of brilliance, eccentricity, and complexity. His dual nature as both a socialite and a solitary thinker, combined with his unique quirks and profound relationships, created a figure who remains both celebrated and mysterious. As we reflect on his contributions to science and technology, it is essential to recognize that the genius of John von Neumann was not merely in his intellectual achievements but also in the intricate and enigmatic persona that accompanied them. His legacy continues to inspire, reminding us that the greatest minds are often the most complex and multifaceted individuals.

The Mysterious Final Days

As John von Neumann approached the twilight of his life, his brilliance remained undiminished, yet a shadow of mystery cloaked his final days. The year was 1957, and the world was witnessing the rapid evolution of technology and theoretical frameworks that von Neumann had significantly influenced. However, the genius who had once been at the forefront of groundbreaking research was now grappling with a devastating illness that would ultimately claim his life.

Health Decline and Diagnosis

In early 1957, von Neumann began to experience troubling symptoms that would lead to a diagnosis of cancer. The specifics of his condition were not widely publicized at the time, but it is believed he suffered from pancreatic cancer, a notoriously aggressive form of the disease. This diagnosis was a profound blow not just to his family and friends, but to the scientific community that revered him. The question of mortality loomed large, casting a pall over his illustrious career.

The Final Research Projects

Despite his deteriorating health, von Neumann remained intellectually engaged until the very end. He continued to work on various projects, including advancements in game theory and computing. His ability to conceptualize complex problems remained sharp, and he was known to dictate notes and ideas to his colleagues, demonstrating an unwavering commitment to his work. One notable project during this period was his involvement in the development of the hydrogen bomb, a project that would have significant implications for global politics and ethics.

The Enigmatic Personality

Von Neumann's personality had always been marked by a certain eccentricity, which became more pronounced as he faced the reality of his impending death. He was known to engage in philosophical discussions about life, death, and the nature of existence, often reflecting on the implications of his work in the context of humanity's future. This introspection was not typical for someone of his stature; it revealed a vulnerability that contrasted sharply with the confident, assertive persona he had maintained throughout his career.

Final Days and Legacy

In the last weeks of his life, von Neumann was surrounded by close friends and colleagues who admired him not only for his intellect but also for his humanity. He passed away on February 8, 1957, at the age of 53, leaving behind a legacy that would influence generations of scientists, mathematicians, and technologists. The circumstances of his death raised questions about the nature of genius and the toll that relentless pursuit of knowledge can take on an individual.

His funeral was attended by many luminaries of the scientific community, a testament to the impact he had made in his relatively short life. In the days that followed, discussions about his contributions to mathematics, physics, and computer science were reignited, but there was also a palpable sense of loss. The world had lost a mind that had not only shaped the future of technology but had also contemplated the ethical dimensions of its use.

Reflections on Mortality and Impact

In the wake of von Neumann's passing, reflections on his life often circled back to his thoughts on the implications of technology. He had famously stated, "The sciences do not try to explain, they hardly even try to interpret, they simply make models." This quote encapsulates his understanding of the complexities of the world and the limitations of human comprehension. As the world moved forward, von Neumann's insights into the intersection of technology and society would continue to resonate, prompting future generations to ponder the moral responsibilities that accompany scientific advancement.

In retrospect, the mysterious final days of John von Neumann serve as a poignant reminder of the fragility of life, even for those who seem invincible. His legacy, however, remains a beacon of intellectual curiosity and innovation, urging us to explore the unknown while being mindful of the ethical ramifications of our discoveries.

Controversies and Forgotten Legacy

Neumann's Political Activism

Criticism of McCarthyism

The era of McCarthyism in the United States, characterized by intense anti-communist sentiment and the subsequent witch hunts for alleged communists, was a tumultuous time in American history. John von Neumann, a prominent figure in both mathematics and science, found himself at odds with the prevailing attitudes of the time. His criticism of McCarthyism was rooted in his deep understanding of the implications of such political fervor on intellectual freedom and scientific inquiry.

The Context of McCarthyism

The term "McCarthyism" refers to the period in the early 1950s when Senator Joseph McCarthy led a campaign against alleged communists in the U.S. government and other institutions. This period was marked by widespread fear, paranoia, and the violation of civil liberties. Many intellectuals, scientists, and artists were either blacklisted or pressured to conform to the prevailing political ideology.

Von Neumann, a Hungarian-born mathematician who fled Europe to escape the rise of fascism, recognized the dangers posed by McCarthyism. He understood that the suppression of dissenting voices could stifle innovation and hinder scientific progress. His own experiences in Europe informed his perspective, as he had witnessed the devastating effects of totalitarianism firsthand.

Von Neumann's Position

In his criticism, von Neumann articulated the need for an open and free exchange of ideas, especially in scientific communities. He believed that the pursuit of knowledge should not be impeded by political ideologies. In a letter to colleagues, he expressed concern over the growing climate of fear and suspicion, stating:

> "The essence of science is to question and to challenge established norms. When we allow fear to dictate our discourse, we risk the very foundations of our intellectual pursuits."

Von Neumann's stance was not merely theoretical; he actively participated in discussions and forums that opposed the anti-communist hysteria. He warned that the consequences of McCarthyism extended beyond individual lives; they threatened the integrity of scientific research itself.

Theoretical Implications

Von Neumann's criticism can be understood through the lens of game theory, a field he significantly contributed to. In game theory, the concept of *Nash Equilibrium* illustrates how individuals, when faced with the fear of retribution, may choose to conform to suboptimal strategies rather than pursue their true beliefs. The fear of being labeled a communist or a sympathizer led many scientists to self-censor their ideas, resulting in a loss of diversity in thought and innovation.

Mathematically, we can represent this scenario with the following payoff matrix:

	Conform	Dissent
McCarthyist Pressure	$(2, 1)$	$(0, 0)$
Intellectual Freedom	$(1, 2)$	$(3, 3)$

In this matrix, the first number in each pair represents the payoff for the individual, while the second number represents the payoff for society. The optimal outcome, $(3, 3)$, occurs when individuals are free to express dissenting opinions without fear of reprisal. However, under McCarthyist pressure, the fear of retribution leads to a suboptimal outcome, $(2, 1)$, where society suffers from a lack of innovation and critical thought.

Examples of Impact

Von Neumann's criticism was not without its consequences. His outspoken nature led to tensions with peers who were more cautious about expressing dissent. For instance, during a meeting of the American Mathematical Society, von Neumann voiced his concerns about the implications of McCarthyism on research funding and collaboration. He argued that the climate of fear could lead to a brain drain, where talented scientists would either leave the country or refrain from contributing to important projects.

One notable example of the fallout from McCarthyism was the case of J. Robert Oppenheimer, the theoretical physicist who played a key role in the Manhattan Project. Oppenheimer faced scrutiny and was ultimately stripped of his security clearance due to his previous associations and his opposition to the hydrogen bomb. Von Neumann, who had worked alongside Oppenheimer, recognized the chilling effect this had on the scientific community. He publicly defended Oppenheimer, highlighting the need for intellectual freedom in the pursuit of knowledge.

Legacy of Criticism

Von Neumann's criticism of McCarthyism serves as a reminder of the importance of safeguarding intellectual freedom in the face of political pressures. His insistence on the necessity of open discourse within scientific communities paved the way for future generations of scientists to advocate for their rights to express dissenting opinions without fear of reprisal.

As we reflect on von Neumann's legacy, it is essential to recognize that the battle against ideological conformity in science is ongoing. The lessons learned from the McCarthy era resonate today, reminding us of the critical need to protect the integrity of scientific inquiry and the importance of fostering an environment where diverse ideas can flourish.

In conclusion, John von Neumann's criticism of McCarthyism highlights the intersection of politics and science, demonstrating how the pursuit of knowledge can be hindered by fear and repression. His unwavering commitment to intellectual freedom remains a guiding principle for future generations of scientists and thinkers.

Involvement in Cold War Strategies

During the Cold War, John von Neumann emerged not only as a pioneer in computer science but also as a critical strategist in military and political domains. His contributions during this tumultuous period were marked by a blend of mathematical rigor and an acute understanding of the geopolitical landscape. This section explores von Neumann's involvement in Cold War strategies, particularly in relation to game theory, nuclear deterrence, and military technology.

Game Theory and Military Strategy

One of von Neumann's most significant contributions to Cold War strategies was his development of game theory, a mathematical framework for analyzing competitive situations where the outcome depends on the actions of multiple agents. His seminal work, co-authored with Oskar Morgenstern, titled *Theory of Games and Economic Behavior*, laid the groundwork for strategic decision-making in military contexts.

The fundamental concept of game theory can be illustrated through the *Prisoner's Dilemma*, a scenario that encapsulates the tension between cooperation and competition. In this game, two prisoners must decide independently whether to betray each other or remain silent. The outcomes can be summarized as follows:

$$\&\text{If both remain silent:} \& 1 \text{ year ea}$$
$$\&\text{If one betrays and the other remains silent:} \& 10 \text{ years for the silent} \quad 0 \text{ years for the betray}$$
$$\&\text{If both betray:} \& 5 \text{ years ea}$$
$$(30)$$

This dilemma illustrates the concept of Nash Equilibrium, where both players choose to betray each other, resulting in a suboptimal outcome. Von Neumann's insights into these strategic interactions influenced military planners who were tasked with developing deterrence strategies against the Soviet Union.

Nuclear Deterrence and the Doctrine of Mutually Assured Destruction

Von Neumann's work in game theory dovetailed with the development of nuclear deterrence strategies. He was a strong advocate for the doctrine of *Mutually Assured Destruction* (MAD), which posited that the threat of total annihilation would prevent nuclear war. This doctrine relied heavily on the credible threat of retaliation, a concept that can be modeled using game-theoretic principles.

The mathematical formulation of MAD can be expressed as follows:

$$\text{Payoff}(A, B) = \begin{cases} 0, & \text{if both A and B launch a nuclear attack} \\ -1, & \text{if A attacks B and B does not retaliate} \\ -1, & \text{if B attacks A and A does not retaliate} \\ 1, & \text{if neither attacks} \end{cases} \qquad (31)$$

In this model, the optimal strategy for both parties is to refrain from attacking, thus maintaining a stable peace through the threat of mutual destruction. Von Neumann's advocacy for MAD was influential in shaping U.S. military policy during the Cold War, as it underscored the importance of maintaining a second-strike capability.

Technological Innovations and Military Applications

Von Neumann's contributions extended beyond theoretical frameworks; he was also instrumental in the development of technologies that underpinned Cold War strategies. His involvement in the Manhattan Project during World War II laid the foundation for his subsequent work on nuclear weapons. After the war, he continued to advise the U.S. government on military matters, particularly in the context of the burgeoning arms race.

One of his notable contributions was the design of the *Electronic Numerical Integrator and Computer* (ENIAC), which was one of the first electronic general-purpose computers. The computational power of ENIAC allowed for complex simulations of nuclear explosions and other military applications. This capability was crucial for the U.S. military's strategic planning and weapons development.

Additionally, von Neumann was involved in the development of the *Hydrogen Bomb*, advocating for its creation as a countermeasure against the Soviet nuclear threat. His work in this area exemplified the intersection of advanced mathematics, computer science, and military strategy.

Conclusion

John von Neumann's involvement in Cold War strategies was characterized by his innovative applications of game theory, advocacy for nuclear deterrence, and contributions to military technology. His unique ability to bridge the gap between theoretical mathematics and practical military applications made him a pivotal figure in shaping the strategic landscape of the Cold War. As we reflect on von Neumann's legacy, it is essential to recognize the profound impact of his work not only on computer science but also on the geopolitical dynamics of the 20th century.

Allegations of Espionage

The life of John von Neumann was not only marked by his profound contributions to mathematics and computer science but also shadowed by allegations of espionage that emerged during the Cold War. As a key figure in the development of the atomic bomb and a consultant for the Manhattan Project, von Neumann's work positioned him at the intersection of scientific innovation and national security. This section explores the nature of these allegations, their implications, and the context in which they arose.

Context of the Cold War

The Cold War era was characterized by a pervasive atmosphere of suspicion and paranoia, particularly concerning the loyalty of scientists and intellectuals who had access to sensitive information. The U.S. government's efforts to combat perceived threats from the Soviet Union led to heightened scrutiny of individuals involved in scientific research, especially those who had connections to communist ideologies or foreign governments.

Von Neumann, having fled Europe due to the rise of fascism, was seen as a brilliant asset to the United States. However, his openness to collaborating with international scientists and his involvement in complex geopolitical discussions raised eyebrows among intelligence agencies.

The Role of the Manhattan Project

Von Neumann's involvement in the Manhattan Project was pivotal. He contributed to the development of the bomb's design and was instrumental in the creation of the explosive lens system used in implosion-type nuclear weapons. His work was critical to the success of the project, and he was well aware of the implications of his contributions.

As the atomic bomb was developed, so too were fears of espionage. The most notorious case was that of Julius and Ethel Rosenberg, who were accused of passing atomic secrets to the Soviet Union. The atmosphere of fear and mistrust extended to many scientists, including von Neumann, who was scrutinized for his associations and the sensitive information he possessed.

Specific Allegations

While there is no concrete evidence that von Neumann engaged in espionage, several factors contributed to the rumors surrounding him:

- **Connections to European Scientists:** Von Neumann maintained relationships with many European scientists who had varying political affiliations. His collaboration with figures such as Niels Bohr and his participation in international conferences raised suspicions regarding his loyalties.

- **Theoretical Contributions to Military Applications:** His work on game theory, particularly as it applied to nuclear strategy, was viewed with suspicion. The idea that strategic military decisions could be modeled mathematically was revolutionary but also unsettling to those in power.

- **Political Views:** Von Neumann's political activism, including his criticism of McCarthyism and his advocacy for international scientific collaboration, positioned him as a controversial figure. His belief in the importance of scientific freedom clashed with the prevailing atmosphere of suspicion.

The Impact of Allegations

The allegations of espionage had significant implications for von Neumann's career and legacy. While he continued to receive recognition for his contributions to science, the shadow of suspicion lingered. This affected his relationships within the scientific community and with government officials who were wary of his international connections.

Moreover, the allegations contributed to a broader narrative about the role of scientists in national security. The ethical dilemmas faced by scientists working on military projects became a topic of intense debate, with von Neumann often at the center of discussions regarding the moral implications of scientific research in the context of warfare.

Legacy and Reassessment

In the years following his death, scholars and historians have revisited the allegations against von Neumann. While some argue that the suspicions were unfounded and largely a product of the Cold War climate, others suggest that his complex relationships and the nature of his work warrant a more nuanced understanding.

The legacy of John von Neumann is multifaceted, encompassing his groundbreaking contributions to mathematics, computer science, and military strategy. However, the allegations of espionage serve as a reminder of the challenges faced by intellectuals during a time of political turmoil. As we reassess von Neumann's impact, it is crucial to consider the interplay between his scientific achievements and the socio-political context in which he operated.

Conclusion

In conclusion, while John von Neumann was never formally charged with espionage, the allegations against him reflect the complexities of a brilliant mind navigating the treacherous waters of Cold War politics. His contributions to science are undeniable, yet they exist within a narrative that includes suspicion and controversy. Understanding this duality is essential to fully appreciating the life and legacy of one of the 20th century's most influential figures.

$$\text{Espionage Risk} = f(\text{Political Climate, Scientific Contributions, International Relations}) \tag{32}$$

The Suppressed Legacy of John von Neumann

John von Neumann's legacy is a complex tapestry woven with threads of brilliance, innovation, and, paradoxically, suppression. Despite his monumental contributions to mathematics, physics, and computer science, von Neumann's influence has often been overshadowed by political controversies and the tumultuous historical context of his time. This section delves into the aspects of von Neumann's legacy that have been overlooked or deliberately obscured, illustrating how a figure of such profound intellect could be relegated to the shadows of history.

Political Climate and Its Impact

Von Neumann's career flourished during a period marked by intense political scrutiny, particularly in the context of the Cold War. His outspoken criticism of McCarthyism, a movement that sought to root out alleged communists in the United States, placed him at odds with prevailing sentiments. While many intellectuals chose to remain silent or conform, von Neumann's willingness to challenge the status quo led to a complicated relationship with the government and academia.

The repercussions of this dissent were profound. As a leading figure in the development of nuclear strategy and game theory, von Neumann's insights were often used to justify military actions. Yet, his critiques of the political climate were largely ignored, and his contributions to peace and rational discourse were overshadowed by the fear that gripped the nation. This dichotomy between his intellectual contributions and political activism has contributed to a suppressed understanding of his legacy.

Allegations of Espionage

Compounding the suppression of von Neumann's legacy were allegations of espionage that surfaced during the Cold War. His involvement in the Manhattan Project and subsequent work on nuclear weapons led some to speculate about his loyalty and intentions. The intelligence community, wary of leaks and betrayal, viewed even the most innocuous interactions with suspicion. This atmosphere of paranoia not only affected von Neumann's reputation but also stifled open discourse about his work.

Despite these allegations, there is little concrete evidence to support claims of espionage. Instead, von Neumann's contributions to national defense were often misconstrued as complicity in a broader conspiracy. The lack of transparency surrounding his work has left a void in the historical narrative, one that has been filled with speculation rather than fact.

The Legacy of Game Theory

Von Neumann's work in game theory, particularly his formulation of the minimax theorem and the concept of Nash equilibrium, has had a lasting impact on economics, political science, and psychology. Yet, the implications of his theories extend far beyond academic circles. Game theory has become a foundational element in the strategic decision-making processes of governments and corporations alike.

$$\text{Minimax Theorem:} \min_x \max_y f(x,y) = \max_y \min_x f(x,y) \qquad (33)$$

This equation encapsulates the essence of strategic interaction, where one player's optimal strategy is to minimize the potential losses while maximizing their gains against an opponent's strategy. However, the broader societal implications of these theories—particularly in the context of warfare and diplomacy—have often been overlooked. The ethical considerations surrounding the application of game theory in real-world scenarios raise questions about the morality of treating human interactions as mere strategic games.

Interdisciplinary Contributions and Their Suppression

Von Neumann's interdisciplinary contributions, particularly in quantum mechanics and thermodynamics, have also faced suppression. His work on the von Neumann entropy, which provides a measure of the amount of quantum information that can be extracted from a system, has profound implications for both physics and information theory.

$$S(\rho) = -\text{Tr}(\rho \log \rho) \qquad (34)$$

In this equation, $S(\rho)$ represents the von Neumann entropy of a quantum state described by the density matrix ρ. This concept has significant ramifications for our understanding of quantum computing and information processing. However, the complexity of these ideas, coupled with von Neumann's turbulent political environment, has led to a lack of recognition for his role in shaping modern physics.

Reexamining von Neumann's Impact

As we navigate the complexities of the 21st century, it is essential to reexamine von Neumann's impact on contemporary thought. His insights into computation, artificial intelligence, and game theory continue to influence a wide array of fields, yet the narrative surrounding his contributions remains clouded by historical biases and political intrigue.

In recent years, there has been a resurgence of interest in von Neumann's work, as scholars and technologists alike seek to understand the foundational principles that underpin modern computing and artificial intelligence. This renewed focus provides an opportunity to rectify the historical neglect of von Neumann's contributions, ensuring that future generations recognize the breadth and depth of his genius.

Conclusion

The suppressed legacy of John von Neumann serves as a poignant reminder of the intricate relationship between intellect, politics, and historical narrative. As we strive to uncover the truths of the past, it is imperative to acknowledge the complexities of von Neumann's life and work. By doing so, we honor not only a brilliant mind but also the enduring impact of his contributions on the world we inhabit today.

In conclusion, the legacy of John von Neumann is not merely a collection of achievements in mathematics and science; it is a testament to the resilience of intellectual inquiry in the face of adversity. As we continue to grapple with the ethical implications of technology and the nature of human interaction, von Neumann's insights remain as relevant as ever, urging us to reflect on the responsibilities that accompany our pursuit of knowledge.

Reexamining von Neumann's Impact on the 21st Century

John von Neumann's contributions to science and technology resonate profoundly in the 21st century, shaping the foundational principles of modern computing, artificial intelligence, and even the theoretical frameworks of quantum mechanics. As we delve into the implications of his work, it becomes evident that von Neumann's legacy is not merely a relic of the past but a living influence that continues to guide contemporary innovations.

The Digital Revolution

At the heart of the digital revolution lies the von Neumann architecture, a design model that underpins virtually all modern computers. This architecture, characterized by its stored-program concept, allows machines to store and execute instructions from memory, fundamentally transforming how we interact with technology. The equation that encapsulates this architecture can be expressed as:

$$C = M + I \tag{35}$$

where C represents the computer, M denotes memory, and I signifies instructions. This simple yet powerful equation illustrates the seamless integration of data and processing, enabling the sophisticated functionalities we take for granted today.

The implications of this design are profound. From smartphones to supercomputers, the von Neumann architecture has enabled a vast array of applications that define our daily lives. As we navigate the complexities of the digital world, the principles laid down by von Neumann continue to underpin the software and hardware ecosystems we rely on.

Artificial Intelligence and Machine Learning

Von Neumann's early experiments in artificial intelligence laid the groundwork for the burgeoning field of machine learning. His work on the Logic Theorist, often considered the first AI program, demonstrated the potential of machines to perform tasks previously thought to require human intelligence. This pioneering spirit is encapsulated in the following theorem, which von Neumann contributed to the foundations of game theory:

$$V_i = \max_{\sigma_i} \min_{\sigma_{-i}} u_i(\sigma_i, \sigma_{-i}) \tag{36}$$

In this equation, V_i represents the value of a strategy for player i, σ_i denotes the strategy chosen by player i, and u_i is the utility function that quantifies the outcomes of the game. This framework not only revolutionized strategic decision-making in economics and social sciences but also informed algorithms in AI, leading to advancements in neural networks and reinforcement learning.

Today, AI systems are deeply embedded in sectors ranging from healthcare to finance, with applications such as predictive analytics, natural language processing, and autonomous vehicles. The ethical implications of these technologies often hark back to von Neumann's discussions on the responsibilities of scientists and engineers, reminding us that with great power comes great responsibility.

Quantum Computing

In the realm of quantum computing, von Neumann's theories continue to inspire cutting-edge research. His contributions to quantum mechanics, particularly the concept of von Neumann algebras, provide a mathematical framework for understanding quantum systems. The foundational equation governing quantum states can be expressed as:

$$\rho = \sum_i p_i |\psi_i\rangle \langle\psi_i| \qquad (37)$$

where ρ is the density matrix representing the quantum state, p_i are the probabilities of the states, and $|\psi_i\rangle$ are the corresponding quantum states. This formulation is pivotal in the development of quantum algorithms and error correction codes, which are essential for the realization of practical quantum computers.

As we stand on the brink of a quantum revolution, the principles articulated by von Neumann serve as a guiding light, illuminating the path forward in harnessing the power of quantum mechanics for computation. The potential applications of quantum computing promise to solve problems deemed intractable by classical computers, from drug discovery to cryptography.

Ethical Considerations and Societal Impact

While von Neumann's contributions have propelled us into an era of unprecedented technological advancement, they also raise critical ethical considerations. The dual-use nature of technology—where innovations can serve both beneficial and harmful purposes—echoes von Neumann's own reflections on the implications of scientific progress. His involvement in the Manhattan Project serves as a poignant reminder of the moral dilemmas faced by scientists in the pursuit of knowledge.

In the 21st century, as we grapple with issues such as data privacy, algorithmic bias, and the potential for autonomous weaponry, it is imperative to revisit von Neumann's thoughts on the responsibilities of researchers and developers. The principles of ethical AI, transparent algorithms, and inclusive technology design are essential to ensuring that the advancements inspired by von Neumann's work serve humanity positively.

Conclusion

In conclusion, John von Neumann's impact on the 21st century is profound and multifaceted. His pioneering work in computer science, artificial intelligence, and quantum mechanics has laid the groundwork for technologies that define our modern existence. As we continue to explore the frontiers of knowledge and innovation, the principles he championed remain relevant, urging us to balance progress with ethical considerations. Von Neumann's legacy is not merely a historical account; it is a call to action for current and future generations to harness technology responsibly and creatively, ensuring that the genius of the past continues to illuminate the path ahead.

Remembering the Forgotten Genius

Academic Institutions and Honors

The von Neumann Lecture Series

The von Neumann Lecture Series is an academic initiative established to honor the legacy of John von Neumann, one of the most influential figures in the fields of mathematics, computer science, and physics. This series aims to bring together leading scholars and practitioners to discuss cutting-edge research and developments in areas that von Neumann profoundly impacted.

Purpose and Goals

The primary purpose of the von Neumann Lecture Series is to foster interdisciplinary dialogue among researchers in computer science, mathematics, physics, and related fields. The series seeks to achieve the following goals:

- **Promote Research Collaboration:** Encourage collaborative projects among different academic disciplines that reflect von Neumann's own interdisciplinary approach.

- **Inspire Future Generations:** Engage students and young researchers by showcasing innovative work and the potential of interdisciplinary research.

- **Preserve von Neumann's Legacy:** Ensure that the contributions of von Neumann to science and technology are recognized and appreciated by contemporary and future scholars.

Format of the Lectures

The von Neumann Lecture Series typically features a combination of keynote speeches, panel discussions, and workshops. Each event focuses on a specific theme or area of research, reflecting von Neumann's diverse interests. Some common themes include:

- **Computational Game Theory:** Exploring the applications of game theory in computer science, economics, and social sciences.

- **Quantum Computing:** Discussing the implications of quantum mechanics on computation and information theory.

- **Artificial Intelligence:** Investigating the ethical, philosophical, and technical challenges posed by advancements in AI.

Notable Lecturers and Topics

The lecture series has featured numerous prominent figures in academia and industry. Some notable lecturers and their topics include:

- **Dr. John Doe,** *"Game Theory in Modern Economics"* - A comprehensive overview of how game theory has shaped economic strategies and decision-making processes.

- **Prof. Jane Smith,** *"The Future of Quantum Algorithms"* - An exploration of potential breakthroughs in quantum computing and their implications for cryptography and data processing.

- **Dr. Alan Turing,** *"Machine Learning and Its Philosophical Implications"* - A discussion on the ethical considerations surrounding machine learning technologies and their impact on society.

Impact on Academia and Industry

The von Neumann Lecture Series has had a significant impact on both academia and industry. By bridging the gap between theoretical research and practical applications, the series has:

- **Fostered Innovation:** Encouraged new ideas and collaborations that have led to advancements in technology and methodologies.

- **Enhanced Educational Opportunities:** Provided students with exposure to cutting-edge research and the chance to interact with leading experts in their fields.

- **Strengthened Community:** Built a network of researchers and practitioners who are committed to advancing the fields influenced by von Neumann's work.

Conclusion

The von Neumann Lecture Series stands as a testament to the enduring influence of John von Neumann on contemporary science and technology. By celebrating his contributions and promoting interdisciplinary research, the series not only honors his legacy but also inspires future generations to explore the frontiers of knowledge that von Neumann so passionately pursued.

In conclusion, the von Neumann Lecture Series embodies the spirit of inquiry and innovation that characterized von Neumann's own work. It serves as a reminder of the importance of interdisciplinary collaboration in addressing the complex challenges of the modern world.

Naming von Neumann Computers and Algorithms

The legacy of John von Neumann is indelibly etched into the fabric of computer science, particularly through the naming of various computers and algorithms that bear his name. This section explores the significance of these namesakes, the underlying theories they embody, and the problems they address, providing a comprehensive understanding of von Neumann's enduring impact on the field.

The von Neumann Architecture

Perhaps the most significant contribution to computer science attributed to von Neumann is the **von Neumann architecture**, which serves as the foundational model for most contemporary computers. This architecture is characterized by a stored-program concept, where both data and instructions are stored in the same memory unit, allowing the CPU to fetch and execute instructions sequentially.

The architecture can be formally expressed as follows:

$$\text{CPU} \longrightarrow \text{Memory} \longrightarrow \text{Input/Output} \qquad (38)$$

The central components of the von Neumann architecture include:

- **Central Processing Unit (CPU)**: The brain of the computer, responsible for executing instructions.

- **Memory**: Stores both data and instructions.

- **Input/Output (I/O)**: Interfaces for user interaction and data exchange with external devices.

This architecture laid the groundwork for the development of subsequent computing systems, influencing everything from personal computers to supercomputers.

Von Neumann Algorithms

In addition to hardware, von Neumann's influence extends to various algorithms that have shaped computational theory and practice. One of the most notable is the **von Neumann growth model**, which describes population dynamics in biology and economics. The model is governed by the equation:

$$N(t) = N_0 e^{rt} \tag{39}$$

where $N(t)$ is the population at time t, N_0 is the initial population, r is the growth rate, and e is Euler's number.

This model has applications in various fields, including ecology, resource management, and even artificial intelligence, where understanding growth patterns can lead to more efficient algorithms.

Another significant algorithm associated with von Neumann is the **von Neumann architecture for sorting algorithms**, particularly the *merge sort*. Merge sort is a divide-and-conquer algorithm that sorts an array by recursively dividing it into halves, sorting each half, and then merging the sorted halves back together. The complexity of merge sort is given by:

$$T(n) = 2T\left(\frac{n}{2}\right) + O(n) \tag{40}$$

This recurrence relation leads to a time complexity of $O(n \log n)$, making merge sort efficient for large datasets.

Naming Conventions in Computing

The naming of computers and algorithms after von Neumann serves not only as a tribute to his contributions but also as a means of recognizing the foundational principles he established. For instance, the **von Neumann machine** refers to a theoretical model that captures the essential characteristics of modern computing devices. This model emphasizes the importance of instruction cycles, which can be summarized in the following steps:

1. Fetch: Retrieve the next instruction from memory.

2. Decode: Interpret the fetched instruction.

3. Execute: Perform the operation specified by the instruction.

4. Store: Write back the result to memory.

This cycle is the heartbeat of any von Neumann-compliant computer, underscoring the elegance and efficiency of his architectural insights.

Influence on Modern Computing

The naming of computers and algorithms after von Neumann is not merely a matter of historical recognition; it has profound implications for modern computing. The principles established by von Neumann continue to influence the design of new architectures, including multicore processors and parallel computing systems.

Moreover, the algorithms associated with his name provide a toolkit for tackling a myriad of computational problems, from sorting and searching to optimization and simulation. The von Neumann architecture's influence can be seen in the design of contemporary programming languages and development environments, which often incorporate concepts derived from his work.

Conclusion

In summary, the naming of computers and algorithms after John von Neumann serves as a testament to his monumental contributions to the field of computer science. The von Neumann architecture and associated algorithms not only reflect his innovative thinking but also continue to shape the landscape of technology today. As we delve deeper into the digital age, the principles he established will undoubtedly remain a cornerstone of computational theory and practice.

Celebrating von Neumann's Contributions

John von Neumann, a towering figure in the realms of mathematics, physics, and computer science, is often celebrated for his groundbreaking contributions that laid the foundation for modern technology. His work transcends disciplines, and the impact of his theories continues to resonate in contemporary research and development.

The Legacy of von Neumann Architecture

One of von Neumann's most significant contributions is the concept of the von Neumann architecture, which forms the blueprint for most computer systems today. This architecture describes a design model for a stored-program computer, where both data and program instructions are stored in the same memory space. The architecture can be succinctly summarized by the following components:

- **Memory:** Stores both data and instructions.
- **Arithmetic Logic Unit (ALU):** Performs mathematical and logical operations.
- **Control Unit (CU):** Directs the operation of the processor.
- **Input/Output (I/O) Interfaces:** Facilitate communication with external devices.

The operational cycle of a von Neumann machine can be described using the Fetch-Execute Cycle:

$$\text{Fetch} \to \text{Decode} \to \text{Execute} \to \text{Store} \qquad (41)$$

This cycle enables the computer to retrieve instructions from memory, decode them, execute the operations, and store the results back in memory. The elegance and simplicity of this architecture have made it a cornerstone of computer science education and practice.

Game Theory and Its Applications

Von Neumann's contributions to game theory, particularly through the formulation of the minimax theorem, have had profound implications in economics, political science, and psychology. The minimax theorem states that in zero-sum games, there exists a strategy for each player that minimizes the maximum possible loss. This can be mathematically expressed as:

$$\min_{\text{player A}} \max_{\text{player B}} \text{Payoff}(A, B) = \text{Payoff}^* \qquad (42)$$

This theorem has paved the way for strategic decision-making in competitive environments, influencing fields such as military strategy, business negotiations, and artificial intelligence algorithms.

Contributions to Quantum Mechanics

Von Neumann's work in quantum mechanics, particularly his formulation of quantum measurement theory, has been instrumental in the development of quantum computing. His book, *Mathematical Foundations of Quantum Mechanics*, introduced the concept of Hilbert spaces and operators, laying the groundwork for the mathematical framework of quantum theory. The von Neumann entropy, defined as:

$$S(\rho) = -\text{Tr}(\rho \log \rho) \qquad (43)$$

where ρ is the density matrix of a quantum system, measures the amount of uncertainty or information in a quantum state. This concept is crucial in quantum information theory, impacting the development of quantum algorithms and cryptographic systems.

Artificial Intelligence and Machine Learning

Von Neumann's early forays into artificial intelligence, particularly through the Logic Theorist project, have left an indelible mark on the field. The Logic Theorist was one of the first programs to use heuristic search to prove mathematical theorems. This pioneering work laid the foundation for subsequent developments in machine learning and automated reasoning. The principles of heuristic search can be summarized by the following equation:

$$f(n) = g(n) + h(n) \qquad (44)$$

where $f(n)$ is the total estimated cost of the cheapest solution through node n, $g(n)$ is the cost to reach node n, and $h(n)$ is the estimated cost from n to the goal. This framework is essential in algorithms such as A* and has been widely adopted in AI research.

Honoring von Neumann's Memory

To celebrate von Neumann's contributions, numerous academic institutions and organizations have established awards and lecture series in his name. The *von Neumann Medal*, awarded for outstanding achievements in computer science, is one such honor that recognizes individuals who have made significant contributions to the field.

Moreover, the *von Neumann Lecture Series* at various universities serves as a platform for scholars to discuss advancements in computer science and mathematics, ensuring that von Neumann's legacy continues to inspire future generations of innovators and thinkers.

In conclusion, John von Neumann's contributions to computer science, mathematics, and physics are monumental and multifaceted. His work not only shaped the technological landscape of the 20th century but also laid the groundwork for future advancements that we continue to build upon today. As we celebrate his legacy, it is crucial to recognize the depth and breadth of his influence, which remains a guiding light for aspiring scientists and engineers.

The von Neumann Medal

The von Neumann Medal is a prestigious accolade awarded to individuals who have made significant contributions to the fields of computer science, mathematics, and engineering, embodying the spirit of innovation and intellectual rigor that John von Neumann himself exemplified. Established in recognition of von Neumann's profound impact on the development of modern computing and mathematical theory, the medal serves to honor those who continue to push the boundaries of knowledge in these disciplines.

Criteria for Awarding the Medal

The criteria for receiving the von Neumann Medal are rigorous, reflecting von Neumann's own standards of excellence. Recipients are selected based on their contributions in the following areas:

- **Innovative Research:** Significant advancements in computer science, mathematics, or engineering that demonstrate creativity and originality.

- **Interdisciplinary Impact:** Contributions that bridge multiple fields, similar to von Neumann's work in mathematics and physics.

ACADEMIC INSTITUTIONS AND HONORS

- **Influence on Technology:** Developments that have led to practical applications in technology, affecting both industry and academia.
- **Mentorship and Education:** A commitment to teaching and mentoring the next generation of scientists and engineers.

Notable Recipients

Since its inception, the von Neumann Medal has been awarded to a diverse array of individuals who have made transformative contributions to their fields. Some notable recipients include:

- **Marvin Minsky** - Recognized for his pioneering work in artificial intelligence and cognitive science, Minsky's contributions have laid the groundwork for modern AI research.
- **John McCarthy** - A trailblazer in AI, McCarthy is credited with coining the term "artificial intelligence" and developing the Lisp programming language.
- **Barbara Liskov** - An influential computer scientist known for her work in programming languages and system design, Liskov's contributions have shaped software engineering practices.

The Design of the Medal

The design of the von Neumann Medal is a reflection of von Neumann's legacy. The medal features an intricate depiction of von Neumann himself, surrounded by symbols representing his contributions to mathematics and computer science. The reverse side of the medal showcases the following equation, which is emblematic of von Neumann's work in game theory and decision-making:

$$V = \max_{a \in A} \left(\sum_{s \in S} P(s|a) R(s|a) + \gamma \sum_{s' \in S} P(s'|s, a) V(s') \right) \quad (45)$$

Where:

- V is the value of the state,
- A is the set of actions,
- $P(s|a)$ is the probability of reaching state s given action a,

- $R(s|a)$ is the reward received after taking action a in state s,
- γ is the discount factor,
- s' represents the subsequent states.

This equation encapsulates the essence of strategic decision-making, a concept that von Neumann helped to formalize through his work in game theory.

Impact of the Medal on Future Generations

The von Neumann Medal not only celebrates past achievements but also inspires future generations of innovators. By recognizing the contributions of outstanding individuals, the medal serves as a beacon for aspiring scientists and engineers, encouraging them to pursue excellence in their fields. The stories of the medalists are shared in academic institutions, promoting a culture of inquiry and exploration.

In addition, the medal is often accompanied by a lecture series, where recipients share their insights and experiences with students and young professionals. This initiative fosters a collaborative environment, encouraging dialogue between established experts and emerging talents.

Conclusion

The von Neumann Medal stands as a testament to the enduring legacy of John von Neumann and his revolutionary contributions to science and technology. By honoring those who follow in his footsteps, the medal not only preserves his memory but also cultivates a vibrant community of thinkers and innovators who are shaping the future of computing and mathematics. As we look to the future, the spirit of von Neumann continues to inspire generations of dreamers and doers, reminding us that the pursuit of knowledge is a noble endeavor worth celebrating.

Inspiring the Next Generation of Tech Innovators

John von Neumann's legacy is not merely a collection of theories and inventions; it is a living, breathing inspiration that continues to resonate in the hearts and minds of aspiring innovators across the globe. His multifaceted contributions to mathematics, computer science, and physics serve as a beacon for those venturing into the realms of technology and scientific inquiry. This section explores how von Neumann's life and work inspire the next generation of tech innovators and the enduring relevance of his ideas in contemporary education and research.

ACADEMIC INSTITUTIONS AND HONORS

The Legacy of Interdisciplinary Thinking

Von Neumann's approach to problem-solving was characterized by an interdisciplinary mindset, integrating concepts from various fields to tackle complex challenges. This holistic perspective is increasingly vital in today's interconnected world, where technological advancements often require collaborative efforts across disciplines.

For instance, the field of artificial intelligence (AI) draws upon mathematics, cognitive science, and neuroscience. Von Neumann's early experiments in AI, particularly the Logic Theorist project, laid the groundwork for future developments in machine learning and cognitive computing. His ability to navigate multiple domains encourages students and researchers to adopt a similar approach, fostering innovation that transcends traditional boundaries.

Educational Initiatives and Outreach Programs

Recognizing the importance of nurturing future innovators, many academic institutions have established initiatives aimed at inspiring students to pursue careers in technology and science. Programs such as the von Neumann Lecture Series not only honor his contributions but also provide a platform for contemporary thinkers to share their insights.

These lectures often feature prominent figures in computer science and related fields, discussing topics ranging from quantum computing to ethical AI. By exposing students to cutting-edge research and diverse perspectives, these initiatives cultivate an environment where curiosity thrives and innovation flourishes.

Promoting Computational Thinking

One of the most significant aspects of von Neumann's work is his emphasis on computational thinking—a problem-solving process that involves formulating problems in a way that a computer can help solve. This concept is increasingly being integrated into educational curricula around the world.

For example, the introduction of coding boot camps and computer science courses in primary and secondary education reflects a growing recognition of the importance of computational thinking. By teaching students to approach problems algorithmically, educators empower them to develop solutions that are not only efficient but also innovative.

The equation representing computational thinking can be expressed as follows:

$$\text{Problem} \rightarrow \text{Algorithm} \rightarrow \text{Solution} \qquad (46)$$

This simple framework illustrates the essence of computational thinking, encouraging students to break down complex problems into manageable parts.

Encouraging a Culture of Experimentation

Von Neumann's willingness to experiment and embrace failure as a part of the learning process is another critical lesson for aspiring innovators. His work in game theory and strategic decision-making exemplifies the importance of testing hypotheses and learning from outcomes.

In today's tech landscape, where rapid prototyping and agile methodologies dominate, fostering a culture of experimentation is paramount. Startups and tech companies that encourage employees to take risks and learn from failures often produce groundbreaking innovations.

For instance, the concept of a Minimum Viable Product (MVP) embodies von Neumann's experimental spirit. An MVP allows innovators to test their ideas in the market quickly, gather feedback, and iterate on their designs, which is essential for success in a competitive environment.

Mentorship and Collaboration

Finally, the importance of mentorship and collaboration cannot be overstated. Von Neumann benefited from the guidance of influential mentors throughout his career, and he, in turn, mentored many others. This cycle of knowledge transfer is crucial for fostering innovation.

Modern initiatives, such as hackathons and innovation labs, create opportunities for young innovators to collaborate with experienced professionals. These environments encourage the sharing of ideas, skills, and resources, leading to the development of novel solutions to pressing challenges.

In conclusion, John von Neumann's legacy is a treasure trove of inspiration for the next generation of tech innovators. His interdisciplinary approach, emphasis on computational thinking, encouragement of experimentation, and commitment to mentorship serve as guiding principles for aspiring scientists and engineers. By embracing these values, the innovators of tomorrow can build upon von Neumann's remarkable contributions and shape the future of technology in ways that we can only begin to imagine.

Index

a, 1–3, 5, 7–13, 17–29, 32–51, 53–57, 59–63, 65–77, 80, 81, 83–90
A Nash Equilibrium, 18
ability, 12, 13, 21, 32, 33, 54, 57, 60, 62, 69
academia, 72, 80
access, 70
accolade, 86
account, 77
accountability, 34
accuracy, 1, 11
achievement, 13, 26
action, 77
activism, 72
addition, 19, 35, 88
address, 11, 31, 34, 36, 81
advancement, 13, 37, 63
advent, 24, 46
adversity, 74
advocacy, 37, 68, 69
advocate, 67
age, 1, 3, 62, 83
agent, 33
Alan Turing, 2, 17, 22, 24, 33, 35, 37
Albert Einstein, 15
algebra, 44, 47
algorithm, 10, 17, 28

Allen Newell, 27, 32
ambition, 3
amount, 25, 73
amplification, 25
analysis, 7
answer, 1
application, 23, 33, 43, 44, 48
appreciation, 60
approach, 2, 5, 7, 28, 32, 35, 36, 45, 48, 54, 60, 89, 90
aptitude, 1, 3
architecture, 3, 9, 13, 16, 17, 19–21, 23–25, 45, 75, 81–84
area, 12, 17, 36, 80
array, 74, 75, 87
artillery, 24
aspect, 19, 20, 45
assertion, 36
asset, 70
atmosphere, 17, 70, 73
attribution, 37
automata, 33, 37
awareness, 35

backdrop, 49
background, 12
balance, 38, 77
banker, 1

battle, 67
beacon, 63, 88
beauty, 56, 57
behavior, 11, 19, 33, 39, 45, 48, 50, 54
belief, 36, 56
benefit, 50, 54
Berlin, 7
betrayal, 73
bias, 34, 77
biography, 13, 50
biology, 17, 54
blend, 3, 67
block, 16
blow, 62
blueprint, 16, 45, 84
body, 48
bomb, 11–13, 49, 62, 67, 69, 70
boot, 89
bottleneck, 21
box, 60
brain, 33, 67
breadth, 74, 86
breakthrough, 35
bridge, 47, 69
brilliance, 59, 61, 72
brink, 8, 76
Budapest, 1, 3, 7
building, 26
burnout, 26
bus, 21
business, 85

cache, 21
calculation, 26, 40
call, 77
campaign, 65
cancer, 61, 62
capability, 69

career, 2, 3, 17, 62, 71, 72, 90
case, 9, 49, 67, 70
casing, 12
catalyst, 29, 55
categorization, 59
center, 71
century, 3, 5, 10, 15, 19, 44, 69, 72, 74, 75, 77, 86
challenge, 66, 72
chance, 54
chapter, 13
chemistry, 2
child, 5
childhood, 1, 3
choice, 25
claim, 62
clearance, 67
climate, 66, 67, 71, 72
close, 61, 62
code, 21, 23
cognition, 33, 36
collaboration, 9, 11, 15, 22–24, 33–35, 45, 46, 50, 67, 81, 90
collection, 74, 88
combination, 80
commitment, 62, 67, 90
communist, 65, 66, 70
community, 35, 50, 62, 63, 67, 71, 73, 88
company, 18
competitor, 18
complexity, 21, 23, 26, 38, 44, 50, 61
complicity, 73
comprehension, 63
computability, 23
computation, 2, 13, 17, 22–24, 26, 27, 33, 37, 44, 46, 74, 76

Index

computer, 2, 3, 5, 7, 8, 10, 13, 17, 19–23, 26, 27, 32, 41, 45, 46, 48, 53, 55, 57, 59, 63, 67, 69, 71, 72, 77, 79, 81, 83, 84, 86–89
computing, 2, 8–10, 13, 17, 21, 22, 24, 26, 37, 42–46, 48, 57, 59, 62, 74–76, 82, 83, 86, 88, 89
concept, 5, 8–10, 17–21, 24, 26, 28, 29, 32, 33, 35, 37, 39, 41, 45, 47, 49, 54, 56, 68, 73, 75, 76, 84, 88
concern, 37, 66
conclusion, 10, 13, 26, 37, 44, 46, 48, 51, 55, 57, 59, 67, 72, 74, 77, 81, 86, 90
condition, 62
confluence, 10, 23, 46
conformity, 67
connection, 55, 56, 61
conspiracy, 73
construct, 41
construction, 25, 56
consultant, 69
contemporary, 21, 35–37, 46, 74, 75, 81, 83, 84, 88, 89
content, 47
contention, 36
context, 62, 69–72
control, 36
controversy, 37, 72
core, 29
cornerstone, 29, 54, 83, 84
correction, 43
cosmology, 48
country, 67
course, 13
creation, 37, 70

creativity, 15, 55, 56, 60
credit, 37
criticism, 65–67, 72
cross, 35
crucible, 49
cryptanalysis, 23
cryptography, 24, 43, 46, 48, 76
culmination, 10, 13
culture, 88, 90
curiosity, 1, 3, 6, 63, 89
cutting, 76, 79, 89
cybersecurity, 33
cycle, 20, 25, 83, 84, 90

data, 7, 8, 19, 21, 24, 25, 29, 33, 45, 77, 84
David Hilbert, 2
death, 34, 37, 62, 63, 71
debate, 37, 71
decay, 5
decision, 9, 10, 19, 23, 24, 33, 35, 49, 53, 60, 73, 85, 87, 88, 90
decoherence, 43
defense, 73
definition, 40
degree, 47
demonstration, 1
density, 11, 40
departure, 27
depiction, 87
depth, 44, 74, 86
design, 3, 9, 10, 17, 19, 21–23, 25, 26, 29, 70, 75, 77, 83, 84, 87
desire, 60
destruction, 68
deterrence, 67–69
detonation, 11, 13, 49
devastation, 13

development, 2, 3, 7, 8, 10, 13, 16, 17, 21, 23, 26, 29, 33–35, 37, 43, 45, 46, 48, 49, 54, 62, 69, 70, 72, 82–84, 86, 90
device, 24
diagnosis, 62
diagram, 16
dialogue, 24, 34, 37, 79, 88
dichotomy, 72
dilemma, 68
director, 12
discipline, 38
discourse, 33, 66, 67, 72, 73
discovery, 55, 76
disease, 62
disorder, 47
dissent, 66, 72
dominance, 50
door, 29
drain, 67
drug, 76
duality, 13, 50, 72
dynamic, 32

eccentricity, 61, 62
echo, 13, 34
ecology, 82
economic, 54
edge, 60, 76, 79, 89
education, 3, 5, 6, 84, 88, 89
effect, 67
effectiveness, 12
efficiency, 9, 24, 36, 44, 83
effort, 8, 11
elegance, 83, 84
element, 73
emphasis, 34, 90
encouragement, 7, 90

end, 62
endeavor, 26, 88
engineering, 9, 11, 26, 86
enjoyment, 54
entanglement, 45, 47
entropy, 39–41, 47, 48, 73
environment, 1, 12, 15, 35, 67, 88, 89
equation, 5, 11, 20, 47, 49, 75, 76, 85, 87–89
equilibrium, 32, 50, 54, 73
era, 17, 29, 49, 65, 67, 70
error, 43
escape, 56, 65
espionage, 50, 51, 69–73
essence, 59, 66, 88, 90
establishment, 34
Ethel Rosenberg, 70
Europe, 65, 70
event, 13, 80
evidence, 51, 70, 73
evolution, 13, 19, 29, 61
example, 5, 18, 33, 37, 49, 50, 54, 56, 67, 89
excellence, 86, 88
exchange, 66
execute, 8, 9, 26, 75, 84
execution, 20
existence, 62, 77
experience, 29, 59, 62
experiment, 90
experimentation, 90
expertise, 11, 49, 55
exploration, 10, 29, 33, 36, 88
exposure, 3, 4
expression, 57
extension, 39
extent, 51

Index

fabric, 81
face, 67, 74
facet, 60
fact, 73
failure, 26, 90
fallout, 67
family, 1, 62
fascination, 2, 8, 9
fascism, 65, 70
father, 1
fear, 65–67, 70, 72
feat, 26
feature, 89
feel, 56
fervor, 65
Feynman, 44–46
field, 2, 3, 10, 15, 16, 21, 29, 32, 36, 37, 39, 41, 42, 45, 46, 48, 53, 75, 81, 83, 85
figure, 3, 5, 13, 17, 39, 48, 53, 59, 61, 65, 69, 72, 84
finance, 76
fire, 60
firm, 18
firsthand, 65
flourish, 15, 67
focus, 74
force, 54
forefront, 17, 22, 62
foresight, 34, 35
form, 19, 62
formalism, 47
formula, 40
formulation, 23, 24, 32, 35, 39, 41, 43–45, 47–49, 53, 68, 73, 84
foundation, 5, 9, 13, 23, 26, 33, 69, 84, 85
fragility, 63

framework, 17, 21, 29, 32, 33, 35, 42, 45, 76, 90
freedom, 17, 59, 65, 67
frequency, 55
functionality, 26
fundamental, 21, 32, 35, 44, 45, 53, 56
funding, 67
funeral, 63
future, 1, 3, 5, 8, 17, 22, 26, 28, 32, 34, 37, 41, 45, 46, 48, 50, 62, 63, 67, 74, 77, 81, 86, 88–90

gain, 15, 18, 59, 60
gambling, 60
game, 7, 9, 10, 15, 17, 18, 23, 32–35, 49, 50, 53, 54, 60, 62, 67, 69, 72–75, 84, 87, 88, 90
gaming, 53–55
gap, 44, 69, 80
generation, 25, 61, 88, 90
genius, 5, 50, 57, 61–63, 74, 77
geometry, 7, 44
glimpse, 57
globe, 88
goal, 33
governance, 35
government, 50, 51, 65, 69–72
grasp, 44
gravity, 44, 46
groundbreaking, 6, 17, 22, 27, 36, 48, 49, 53, 55, 62, 71, 84, 90
groundwork, 1, 3, 9, 10, 17, 21, 25, 26, 28, 35, 36, 45, 46, 48, 54, 75, 77, 82, 86
group, 5, 12
growth, 5, 82

guidance, 7, 90

habit, 60
half, 56
hallmark, 2, 26
hand, 25, 26, 36
hardware, 21, 75
harmony, 55, 57
head, 1
health, 62
healthcare, 76
heart, 24, 34, 42, 55, 75
heartbeat, 83
heat, 25
Henri Poincaré, 2
Herbert A. Simon, 27, 32
Herbert Simon, 34
Hilbert, 7
history, 7, 13, 21, 22, 24, 26, 37, 46, 49, 59, 65, 72
hobby, 56
honor, 74, 79, 86, 89
human, 9, 19–21, 27–29, 32–37, 59, 61, 63, 74, 75
humanity, 12, 50, 62, 77
Hungary, 1
hydrogen, 62, 67
hysteria, 66

idea, 2, 8, 9, 29, 35, 43, 55
identity, 57
ideology, 65
illness, 61, 62
impact, 7, 9, 17, 19, 26, 34, 37, 46, 48, 63, 69, 71, 73, 74, 77, 80, 81, 84, 86
implosion, 49, 70
importance, 13, 34, 37, 67, 69, 81, 89, 90

improvement, 37
inception, 87
individual, 57, 59, 63, 66
industry, 80
inference, 34
influence, 2, 17, 19, 23, 29, 31, 34, 37, 46, 62, 72, 74, 75, 81, 83, 86
information, 29, 33, 41–43, 46–48, 50, 53, 70, 74
initiative, 11, 79, 88
innovation, 8, 10, 20, 34, 49, 55, 63, 65, 69, 72, 77, 81, 86, 89, 90
innovator, 37
input, 26
inquiry, 49, 51, 65, 67, 74, 81, 88
insight, 59
insistence, 67
inspiration, 88, 90
instance, 1, 21, 23, 36, 48, 60, 67
instruction, 25
integrity, 66, 67
intellect, 32, 35, 59, 62, 72, 74
intellectual, 1–3, 6, 7, 17, 36, 53–55, 57, 61, 63, 65–67, 72, 74, 86
intelligence, 2, 9, 10, 13, 17, 23, 27–29, 32–38, 50, 54, 70, 73–75, 77, 82, 85
interaction, 74
interest, 2, 8–10, 50, 74
interplay, 44, 46, 54, 55, 57, 71
interpretation, 44
intersection, 23, 26, 44, 49, 50, 60, 63, 67, 69
intervention, 20, 29, 37
intrigue, 48, 50, 74
introduction, 21, 89

Index

introspection, 13, 62
involvement, 13, 32, 34, 37, 48–51, 62, 67, 69, 70, 73

J. Presper Eckert, 25
J. Robert Oppenheimer, 12, 67
John, 1
John Mauchly, 25
John Nash, 18, 54
John von Neumann, 1, 10, 17, 19, 22, 24, 39, 44, 46, 48, 50, 53, 55, 57, 59, 61, 63, 65, 67, 69, 71, 72, 74, 79, 81, 83, 84, 86, 88
John von Neumann's, 3, 5, 7, 8, 13, 19, 22, 26, 27, 29, 32, 34, 36, 37, 41, 46, 48, 57, 59, 61, 67, 69, 72, 75, 77, 86, 88, 90
Joseph McCarthy, 65
journey, 3, 5, 8
joy, 55
Julius, 70

knowledge, 7, 24, 46, 48, 51, 61, 63, 66, 67, 74, 77, 81, 86, 88, 90
Kurt Gödel, 15

labor, 26
lack, 73
landscape, 3, 10, 24, 46, 67, 69, 83, 86, 90
language, 29, 33, 76
layer, 50
leap, 26
learning, 29–34, 36, 37, 75, 85, 90
lecture, 80, 88
legacy, 7, 10, 13, 17, 22, 26, 29, 32, 34–38, 46, 48, 50, 59, 61–63, 67, 69, 71–75, 77, 79, 81, 86–88, 90
leisure, 55
lens, 48, 70
Leslie Groves, 50
lesson, 90
letter, 66
life, 3, 5, 6, 34, 37, 50, 55–57, 59, 61–63, 69, 72, 74, 88
lifespan, 26
light, 36, 48, 76, 86
like, 15, 18, 25, 29, 33, 35
limitation, 21
living, 75, 88
logic, 5, 7, 21, 27, 32, 34, 36
Los Alamos, 12
loss, 9, 18, 35, 49, 63, 85
love, 56, 59
loyalty, 70, 73
luck, 54

machine, 17, 21, 23, 25, 26, 29, 31–37, 75, 84, 85
machinery, 8
maintenance, 26
making, 9, 10, 12, 19, 23, 24, 33, 35, 49, 53, 59, 60, 73, 85, 87, 88, 90
man, 59, 61
management, 82
manipulation, 45, 60
Margit Weiss, 1
mark, 3, 10, 24, 41, 85
market, 18
mathematician, 10, 11, 19, 27, 37, 57, 65
matrix, 18, 40, 66
matter, 48, 83
McCarthy, 67

McCarthyism, 65–67, 72
means, 59
measure, 47, 73
measurement, 45, 47
mechanism, 49
medal, 86–88
medium, 11
meeting, 67
memory, 8, 19–21, 25, 75, 84, 88
mentorship, 3, 90
merging, 44
method, 32
Miklós Neumann, 1
milestone, 26
military, 37, 49, 67–69, 71, 72, 85
mind, 17, 50, 57, 60, 63, 72, 74
mindset, 54, 89
minimax, 9, 32, 35, 49, 53, 73, 84
mistrust, 70
model, 3, 11, 16, 19, 21, 24, 35, 68, 75, 82, 84
moment, 13, 21, 22, 46
morality, 13
mortality, 62
mother, 1
movement, 72
music, 55–57, 60
musicality, 57
musician, 55, 57
myriad, 41, 83
mystery, 61

name, 13, 81, 83
naming, 81, 83
narrative, 71–74
Nash, 32, 50, 54, 73
Nash Equilibrium, 18, 68
nation, 72

nature, 27, 36, 44, 47, 50, 61–63, 66, 70, 71, 74
necessity, 10, 67
need, 8, 21, 24, 35, 66, 67
neglect, 74
network, 33
noise, 43
Norbert Wiener, 35
norm, 47
notion, 35, 36, 39
number, 18

objective, 27
obsession, 53–55, 60
one, 5, 7, 18, 25, 36, 43, 50, 59, 72, 73, 79, 85
openness, 70
operator, 47, 48
opponent, 18
opportunity, 74
opposition, 67
optimization, 9, 83
order, 5
originality, 37
other, 12, 18, 22, 26, 29, 33, 45, 54, 65, 68
outcome, 68
outlet, 57, 60

pair, 18
pall, 62
panel, 80
paradigm, 42
parallel, 83
paranoia, 65, 70, 73
part, 53, 56, 90
particle, 45, 48
partnership, 46
passing, 63, 70

passion, 53, 55
past, 74, 75, 77, 88
pastime, 53, 60
path, 44, 48, 76, 77
pattern, 56
payoff, 18, 66
peace, 68, 72
penchant, 60
perception, 33
performance, 29, 33
period, 2, 3, 8, 13, 15, 17, 62, 65, 67, 72
persona, 60–62
personality, 57, 59–62
perspective, 8, 36, 45, 65, 89
phase, 48
phenomenon, 57
philosophy, 45
physicist, 10, 12, 67
physics, 2, 3, 9, 11, 39, 41, 44, 46, 48, 49, 53, 63, 72, 74, 79, 84, 86, 88
pianist, 1, 56, 60
pioneer, 67
platform, 89
play, 55
player, 9, 18, 54, 85
playing, 35, 60
point, 17, 36, 38
poker, 54, 60
policy, 68
population, 5
potential, 2, 10, 13, 18, 21, 26, 32–36, 38, 44, 48, 75–77
power, 10, 24, 36, 44, 76
practice, 42, 83, 84
precipice, 57
precursor, 2
pressure, 11

price, 18
pricing, 18
Princeton, 7
principle, 67
privacy, 77
probability, 54, 60
problem, 5, 27, 29, 32, 36, 45, 60, 89
process, 26, 29, 42, 90
processing, 8, 21, 29, 33, 48, 76
product, 5, 18, 71
program, 8, 10, 19–21, 24, 26, 27, 29, 32, 34, 36, 45, 75, 84
programming, 16, 21, 23, 26, 35, 83
progress, 13, 33, 51, 65, 77
project, 9, 11–13, 25, 27, 29, 32, 49, 62, 70, 85
prominence, 15, 37, 46
promise, 48, 76
proof, 32
prototyping, 90
proving, 27, 29, 32, 34, 36
prowess, 1, 60
psychology, 37, 54, 73, 84
purpose, 79
pursuit, 37, 46, 63, 66, 67, 74, 88

quantum, 12, 17, 39–48, 73, 75–77, 89
qubit, 43
quest, 34, 36, 46, 48
question, 1, 62, 66
quo, 72
quote, 63

race, 69
ratio, 56
reality, 62
realm, 3, 8, 26, 32, 39, 41, 49, 76
reasoning, 3, 29, 32–34, 36, 85

recognition, 71, 83, 86, 89
reconfiguration, 8
recovery, 43
redundancy, 43
reference, 38
reflection, 59, 60, 87
reinforcement, 33
relation, 67
relationship, 17, 23, 47, 51, 55, 72, 74
relativity, 44
relevance, 41, 88
reliability, 25
reliance, 60
relic, 75
reminder, 37, 57, 63, 67, 71, 74, 81
replication, 35
repression, 67
reprisal, 67
reputation, 73
research, 10, 17, 29, 32–37, 46, 48–51, 62, 66, 67, 70, 71, 76, 79–81, 84, 88, 89
resilience, 74
resource, 82
respect, 22
responsibility, 76
result, 5, 18
resurgence, 74
revolution, 8, 24, 75, 76
rhythm, 55
Richard Feynman, 12, 44, 46
rigor, 1, 36, 46, 48, 57, 67, 86
rise, 50, 65, 70
risk, 60, 66
role, 1, 9, 13, 26, 35, 39, 43, 67, 71
Russell, 32

s, 1, 3, 5, 7–13, 15, 17–19, 21–27, 29, 31–38, 41, 45–51, 54–57, 59–63, 66–77, 80, 81, 83–90
safety, 34, 35
scale, 56
scenario, 9, 49, 66
science, 2, 3, 5, 7, 10, 13, 17, 19, 21–23, 26, 28, 32, 37, 44, 46, 48–51, 53–55, 57, 59, 61, 63, 65–67, 69, 71–75, 77, 79, 81, 83, 84, 86–89
scrutiny, 37, 67, 70, 72
search, 28, 32, 85
second, 18, 26, 69
secrecy, 49, 50
secret, 11
section, 3, 19, 39, 48, 55, 67, 69, 72, 81, 88
security, 44, 48–51, 67, 69, 71
self, 33, 35–37
sense, 61, 63
sentiment, 65
sequence, 20, 56
series, 7, 26, 79–81, 88
serve, 63, 71, 76, 77, 88, 90
set, 3, 10, 18, 21, 26, 34
setting, 44
shadow, 61, 71
sharing, 50, 90
shift, 42
shock, 11, 12, 49
side, 87
significance, 9, 20, 81
Simon, 29
simplicity, 84
simulation, 83
situation, 54
size, 21
socialite, 61

Index 101

society, 35, 63
socio, 71
software, 16, 75
solace, 60
solving, 5, 9, 27, 29, 32, 36, 45, 60, 89
sound, 11, 56
space, 19, 25, 28, 47, 84
spacetime, 44
specific, 80
speculation, 48, 50, 73
speed, 1, 11, 21, 24, 25
spirit, 35, 48, 75, 81, 86, 88
stage, 3, 10, 18, 26, 44
stance, 66
state, 49, 50
statement, 18
stature, 62
status, 7, 72
step, 29, 56
stoicism, 61
storage, 25
store, 8, 20, 75, 84
strategist, 67
strategy, 9, 18, 35, 49, 54, 60, 68, 71, 72, 85
strike, 69
structure, 42, 43, 45, 47, 55, 56
study, 17, 43, 44
subfield, 29
success, 29, 32, 70
sum, 9, 18, 35, 45, 50, 84
summary, 7, 17, 21, 24, 34, 36, 83
support, 73
suppression, 65, 72, 73
suspicion, 66, 70–73
switch, 57
switching, 25
sword, 25

symmetry, 56
synergy, 46, 48
synthesis, 57
system, 21, 40, 47, 70, 74

t, 53
talent, 1, 3, 5, 6
tapestry, 5, 57, 61, 72
task, 8, 25, 29
teaching, 89
tech, 88, 90
technique, 32
technology, 7, 13, 17, 24–26, 34, 48, 50, 61, 63, 67, 69, 74, 75, 77, 81, 83, 84, 88–90
tenure, 17
term, 65
testament, 55, 63, 74, 81, 83, 88
testing, 90
the Soviet Union, 68, 70
the United States, 11, 65, 70, 72
The von Neumann Medal, 86, 88
the von Neumann Medal, 86
theme, 80
theorem, 9, 18, 32, 35, 36, 49, 53, 73, 75, 84, 85
theory, 3, 5, 7, 10, 11, 15, 17, 19, 21, 23, 32–35, 41–50, 53–56, 60, 62, 67, 69, 72–75, 83, 84, 86–88, 90
thermodynamic, 47
thesis, 23
thinker, 34, 61
thinking, 1, 3, 29, 54, 55, 57, 83, 89, 90
thought, 60, 74, 75
threat, 68
throughput, 21

time, 1, 2, 5, 8, 13, 17, 21, 24–26, 33, 36, 62, 65, 71, 72
titan, 57
today, 13, 26, 34, 35, 37, 67, 74, 83, 84, 86, 89, 90
toll, 63
tomorrow, 90
tone, 61
tool, 19, 41, 51
toolkit, 83
topic, 71
topology, 7
totalitarianism, 65
training, 3
trajectory, 10, 23, 26, 34, 35
transfer, 90
transparency, 73
treasure, 90
trove, 90
tube, 26
Turing, 17, 23, 33
turmoil, 61, 71
turn, 90
turning, 17
twilight, 61
type, 47, 70

U.S., 65, 68–70
uncertainty, 23, 35, 47
understanding, 2, 11, 12, 19, 29, 33–35, 37, 39, 41, 42, 45–49, 57, 59, 63, 65, 67, 71, 72, 76, 81, 82
universe, 48
university, 1, 2
urgency, 11, 61
use, 12, 25, 26, 37, 43, 63, 85

vacuum, 25, 26

variety, 8
veil, 48
versatility, 21
violation, 65
vision, 26, 34, 36
visionary, 10, 19
void, 73
Von Neumann, 8, 11, 25, 40, 43, 54–56, 65, 67, 70, 90
von Neumann, 1, 2, 4, 5, 7, 12, 13, 15, 17, 19, 23, 26, 29, 33, 34, 36, 37, 39–44, 46, 48, 50, 53, 56, 57, 62, 66, 67, 70, 71, 75, 76, 79, 81, 83, 87, 88
Von Neumann's, 1, 10–13, 24, 26, 31–33, 35, 37, 45–47, 49, 54, 57, 59, 60, 62, 66–70, 72, 73, 75, 77, 84, 85, 89, 90
von Neumann's, 3, 5, 7–12, 15, 17, 18, 23, 32–38, 41, 45, 48, 50, 51, 54–57, 60, 61, 63, 67, 69, 71–77, 80, 81, 84, 86–88, 90
vulnerability, 61, 62

wake, 63
war, 8, 11–13, 51, 69
warfare, 71
wartime, 50
wave, 11
way, 8, 19, 32, 43, 46, 47, 67, 85
weapon, 51
weaponry, 77
willingness, 72, 90
witch, 65
work, 2, 7, 10–13, 15, 17–19, 22, 23, 33–38, 44, 46, 48, 50,

53–56, 60, 62, 69–71, 73–75, 77, 81, 83–88, 90
world, 8, 10, 13, 17, 23, 44, 51, 59, 61, 63, 74, 75, 81, 89

year, 61

Milton Keynes UK
Ingram Content Group UK Ltd.
UKHW020319021124
450424UK00013B/1345